GARDEN
WOODWORK
in a
WEEKEND

GARDEN
WOODWORK
in a
WEEKEND

RICHARD BLIZZARD

DAVID & CHARLES

A DAVID & CHARLES BOOK

First published in the UK in 1999

A catalogue record for this book is available from the British Library.

ISBN 0 7153 0820 3

Designed by Casebourne Rose Design Associates
Photography by Alan Duns and Howard Gimber

Printed in Singapore by Imago Publishing Ltd
for
David & Charles
Brunel House
Newton Abbot
Devon

CONTENTS

THE PROJECTS

INTRODUCTION

This book contains a range of projects to suit all skills, and a variety of designs that will fit into any garden, big or small. Avoiding the feared traditional woodworking joints, I have designed the projects so that, armed with a minimum of tools, you can make an immediate start. Although many of them will take more than a day to do, there are some that can be completed in one day, and just one or two that take only a few hours.

It is always advisable to begin with the less complex projects (they all have difficulty ratings – see p8), and in this way both your confidence and your ability will grow. You will discover that once you have acquired a certain skill, such as driving screws into timber or using a saw, this will then be repeated frequently. And, to keep things simple, the complete range of designs in the book are based around a limited number of techniques. However the most important factor in all this is confidence, so let's get started.

Making a Start

A place to work is essential. For many households this will be the garage; there are a few more fortunate people who have a shed. However, there is nothing wrong with setting up in the garden on a fine spring day, on the garden table or a similar surface. A good firm place to put things on is essential; a sheet of plywood on the top of an old table will do well. If you work in the garage, clear a space and set things out neatly. Make sure there is sufficient light and nothing on the floor to trip over.

Using the Book

With each of the projects you will find a cutting list. Copy out this list before you set off to the timber merchant, so that you are aware of what you need when you get there. Don't forget that you will need screws, a water-resistant glue and, when the project is finished, wood preservative.

Each project is accompanied by a clear, 'exploded' construction diagram. Before doing anything else, take time to study this so you know exactly how all the bits fit together. The text gives the running order.

Note: please *do not* change from metric to imperial measurements halfway through the project and then complain that the drawing does not work – you may smile but it does happen.

The Tools

There are two types of tools for woodworking – hand tools and power tools. It is true to say that one cannot really do without the other, however, normally the hand tools can do everything a power tool will do but just a little bit slower.

The following pages list a selection of the hand and power tools I think are useful for woodworking. I do not suggest that you buy them all at once, but a full set is something to aim for. I always use Bosch power tools and mainly Stanley hand tools. You may prefer other makes but these are the ones that I have found to be most suited to the tasks I set them.

LIST OF PROJECTS ACCORDING TO DIFFICULTY RATING

☞

This symbol is used to denote the difficulty rating of the projects. I have graded them from one to four according to how hard they are to construct and the number of techniques needed. This enables you to see, at a glance, how simple or complex you can expect a project to be. Start with the simpler ones and, once you have acquired confidence, progress to those that are more complex. Most projects can be completed in a weekend; some may take two.

1 ☞
Bird Table p76
Obelisk p20
Trellises p42
Trough with Trellis p32

2 ☞ ☞
Archway p52
Box Table p94
Coldframe p58
Garden Bench p104

Garden Bridge p110
Plant Stand p122
Potting Bench p64
Tool Caddy p70
Versailles Tub p26

3 ☞ ☞ ☞
Box Bench p88
Box Chair p94
Étagère p36

4 ☞ ☞ ☞ ☞
Lounger p116
Obelisk (for Versailles Tub) p31
Tool Store p82

TOOLS, MATERIALS AND TECHNIQUES

Hand Tools

THERE ARE SOME WONDERFUL HAND TOOLS THAT HAVE BEEN PASSED DOWN FROM FATHER TO SON, AND IN SOME CASES THESE WILL BE USEFUL FOR THE JOBS YOU ARE GOING TO TACKLE. HOWEVER, THESE OLD TOOLS MUST HAVE BEEN WELL MAINTAINED: IF THE SAW IS BLUNT AND THE CHISELS HAVE BEEN USED TO OPEN PAINT TINS, THEN IT IS SENSIBLE TO THINK ABOUT GETTING SOMETHING NEW. A BLUNT TOOL WILL BE HARD TO WORK WITH AND WILL HAVE TO BE USED WITH AN EXCESS OF FORCE, LEADING TO THE POSSIBILITY OF SLIPS AND DAMAGE – NOT JUST TO THE WORK BUT ALSO TO HANDS AND FINGERS.

SAWS

A sharp handsaw (panel saw) is absolutely essential, and it is probably best to buy the fine-toothed variety. Fine-toothed saws, as the name suggests, cut the timber finely and leave few jagged edges. This is where you will discover a huge technological advance in the form of the Jetcut saws made by Stanley. They have some amazing teeth: they cut in both directions, are specially heat treated so they stay sharp for the life of the saw, and will cut man-made boards. The handle and blade are set at 90 degrees, so the saw also functions as a set square. Cutting through large planks is simplicity itself, with almost no effort required. A note of caution: do make sure that you keep your fingers clear at all times as these saws can inflict very nasty cuts. It is also vital that you do all your cutting using a work surface or bench.

A coping saw has a large arched frame, at the bottom of which a thin blade is fitted. This is tensioned by twisting the handle. With such a narrow blade, which can be rotated in its frame, it is possible to cut out curved and awkward shapes.

As its name implies, the tenon saw was developed specifically for cutting the tenons in mortice and tenon joints. Its short steel blade is clamped on the top by a piece of steel or, in the best saws, brass. This stiffens the blade and makes it a very accurate tool for cutting small sections of timber.

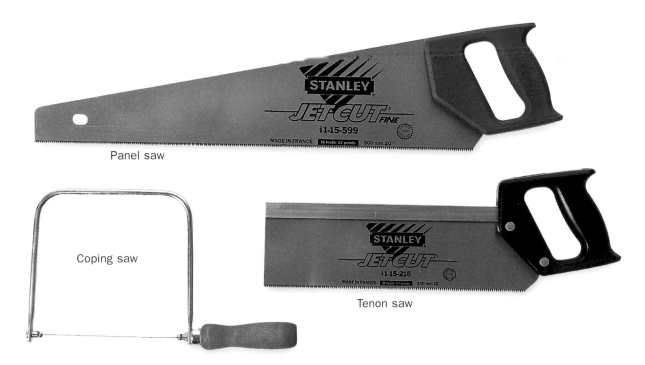

Panel saw

Coping saw

Tenon saw

EXPANDING RULE

An expanding rule provides a quick, efficient method of measuring long lengths of timber. The small hook on the end can be used to hold the rule in place and the lock-off button keeps it extended while you measure off lengths of timber.

DRILL AND ATTACHMENTS

The traditional-design, small hand-drill is still useful to have, but new ones cost more than some of the electric ones that are available. Battery-powered drill/screwdrivers are an excellent choice, see p12.

A selection of different-sized high-speed drill bits is essential. A countersink is also very desirable as it cuts out a recess in the wood, allowing the head of the screw to sit flush with the surface.

Stanley make drill bits called Screw Sinks, which are really the best of both worlds, being a drill plus a countersink on the end. There are different sizes for different gauge screws. These tools speed up boring holes and countersinking tremendously.

SCREWDRIVERS

Today the majority of screws are of the crosshead variety (requiring a Philips or Pozidriv screwdriver). These have become very popular because the cross-shaped slot in the head allows the screwdriver to engage and drive the screw in far more positively, and in some ways more efficiently, than the slot-head type.

The latest Magnum screwdrivers (made by Stanley) have a user-friendly handle: it doesn't give you blisters in the palms of your hand. You will need about three different-sized screwdrivers to cope with the different gauge screws used in the projects.

If you are contemplating driving in dozens of screws, consider buying a Stanley "Yankee" screwdriver which operates with a pump-action. These can be bought in a variety of sizes and have interchangeable heads. A small slider in the side of screwdriver releases a spring-loaded, milled shaft. Once the screw is positioned you literally pump the handle to drive it in.

PLANES

The least expensive types of plane available are the Stanley surform tools, which come in a variety of shapes and sizes. Basically, the steel body holds a sole-plate that has hundreds of pre-sharpened, razor teeth. When sliced along a piece of timber, these teeth quickly shave and reduce the surface.

On the more traditional side, you can also buy a plane that has replaceable, pre-sharpened blades. This eliminates the problem usually experienced with a standard plane, which is that if the blade is not sharp, it will take chunks out of the timber instead of neat shavings. The replaceable-blade plane allows you to slip in a new blade whenever necessary.

HAMMERS

It is best to avoid cheap hammers as the heads may shatter on impact with the nails. Manufacturers such as Stanley x-ray all their hammer heads and any flaws are removed at the manufacturing stage. A good hammer head is fixed to the shaft in such a way that it cannot come off. It is best to buy a hammer with a claw so that nails can be extracted as well as driven in. An ideal weight is about 2lb (1kg).

SAFETY SPECS

It is not unknown for wood chippings to fly up and cause injury to the eyes, especially when using a jigsaw or planer, so safety specs should be worn at all times.

SPIRIT LEVEL

Spirit levels are very useful in all work. Try to get one that not only has a 'bubble' for level, but also a 'bubble' for the 90 degree reading. As long as it has this, a small level will be adequate.

KNIFE

A knife of the Stanley type, with changeable blades, is very useful for woodwork projects. There are a number of patterns available; try to get one with a retractable blade.

CLAMPS

Whenever you are sawing or drilling you must hold the timber down securely. A couple of screw clamps should be sufficient.

CHISELS

A set of three chisels will be adequate for the projects in this book. It is a good idea to buy the shorter-length ones as these are still top quality but they are cheaper.

Those in the Stanley Handyman series have handles made of polypropylene and carbon chrome steel blades, and will, quote, "literally, last you a lifetime of woodworking".

OTHER USEFUL TOOLS

Carpenters generally have a number of gauges, the most useful being a marking gauge and a sliding bevel gauge. The marking gauge has a 'fence' that is adjustable and a small steel spike that marks the wood. Once the fence is set to the correct width, the spiked part of the gauge is 'trailed' along the timber, leaving a line to which you can cut or plane. A sliding

bevel gauge is really a super 90 degree set square. The blade of the gauge can be adjusted to any angle, not just the fixed 90 degrees of the set square.

A small protractor is always useful for checking angles and a compass for marking curves.

Other useful tools include a bradawl, the sharp point of which is used for making a hole in timber to give a starting point for a screw. A small adjustable spanner is invaluable for doing up coach bolts. A set of files is always handy.

It may seem obvious, but you will also need a number of pencils (along with a pencil sharpener), and card for making templates.

POWER TOOLS

A HUGE RANGE OF POWER TOOLS IS AVAILABLE, BUT JUST FOUR ARE NEEDED FOR WORKING THE PROJECTS IN THIS BOOK. I CAN RECOMMEND BOSCH TOOLS. THEY ARE EXTREMELY GOOD VALUE AND WILL GIVE YOU YEARS OF RELIABLE SERVICE. WITH ALL POWER TOOLS, IT IS ESSENTIAL TO READ THE MANUFACTURERS' INSTRUCTIONS CAREFULLY BEFORE STARTING WORK.

Screwdriver and drill
With a battery-powered drill you can undertake any woodworking task in the garden in complete safety.

SCREWDRIVER/DRILL (Battery Powered)

This useful tool has made it possible for the general DIY enthusiast to tackle jobs that might otherwise prove too daunting.

The crucial feature of a battery-powered screwdriver/drill is that it has a slow start. 'Engineered' into the trigger, this enables the operator to start the screwdriver bit turning slowly by squeezing the trigger gently. This allows a screw to be started in the timber and then you can speed up the drill to drive the screw home.

There are two other main functions to look for when buying a battery-powered screwdriver/drill. The first is that it will turn both backwards and forwards, so that screws can be withdrawn as well as inserted. The other is the torque setting. A larger, longer screw requires more torque (turning power) to drive it in than does a smaller, shorter screw, so to achieve this an adjustable clutch is fitted. By turning a ring or other device (according to make and model), it is possible to use it with a variety of screw sizes and lengths, and to set the clutch so that it slips when the screw head is flush with the timber.

The other great advantage of a battery-powered screwdriver/drill is that you can undertake any woodworking or other practical task in the garden

in complete safety, as there is no electric cable to present the potential danger of electrocution on damp or wet days.

Bosch produce a battery-powered screwdriver/drill that fits the bill well. It is not heavy, balances well in the hand, and has sufficient power to drive 4in (10cm) screws straight into pine without the need to bore a pilot hole. It comes with a battery charger and a very useful case, in which spare batteries, drill bits and so on can be kept.

JIGSAW (Mains Powered)

The name of this tool implies that it is something you use to make wooden jigsaw puzzles. No doubt its origins lie here, but today this saw can be used for almost any job that a circular saw or bandsaw can do.

Due to its reciprocal action and, once again, a slow-start facility, this is probably the safest cutting tool available. A wide variety of blades can be purchased, making it possible to cut wood, plastics, chipboard and even mild steel. The jigsaw is also unique in one feature – its ability to cut out internal shapes and holes in wood. A small hole is bored using a drill, the jigsaw blade is inserted and the shape or hole is then cut out.

Do not buy any jigsaw which does not have a small guide wheel at the back of the blade. This wheel has a groove in the centre, and as the blade reciprocates the wheel supports it, thereby taking the strain off the main plunger mechanism.

Some jigsaws have a pendulum action, which when switched on enables the blade to swing (mirroring the action of a hand saw) and cut the timber far more quickly.

Bosch make a jigsaw with all these features that performs cutting operations with great ease.

Mains-powered jigsaw
Due to its reciprocal action and a slow-start facility, this is the safest cutting tool available.

Multi-sander
You can buy random orbital sanders that will produce a first-class finish on wood, paint, brass, copper and plexiglass.

MULTI-SANDER
(Mains Powered)

In order to achieve a good finish on timber, it is important to have a good surface. Endgrain needs to be tidied up and sharp edges removed. You can do all this using a block of cork wrapped with sandpaper, but it will take a long time and you will not be able to achieve as good a finish as you can with a sander.

For many years orbital sanders have served woodworkers well, providing a sanding pad that vibrates at high speed and produces a good surface. Now enter a new generation of 'smoothers' – the random orbital sanders. The most radical way these machines differ from orbital sanders is in the eccentric rotation of the circular sanding pad, which produces a superb surface.

You can buy random orbital sanders that will produce a first-class finish on wood, paint, brass, copper and plexiglass. In the excellent Bosch model, the circular base pad – which can sand successfully on curved surfaces as well as flat – takes sanding sheets with a Velcro-type of fastening, so that they can be changed quickly when worn. You can also choose to fit polishing felt, lambswool fleece or a polishing sponge to the machine. The random orbital sanding/polishing action is adjustable and you can cover large surfaces rapidly. The dust which is produced is sucked up very efficiently into the machine through holes in the sanding disc, and then deposited in a small dust bag.

Until you have tried a random orbital sander, you cannot appreciate just how fast and effective these tools are at smoothing surfaces to a fine finish. The sanding sheets last for a surprisingly long time; working by hand with a cork block and sandpaper may work, but it takes forever, leaves dust everywhere and you will end up using a great deal more sandpaper.

HAND-HELD PLANER (Mains Powered)

You may wonder what relevance a planer has to weekend garden woodworking projects. Quite simply, if you intend to make up a good number of the items, it will save you a great deal of money and time. Two main types of timber are available: sawn and planed (see p15). Planed timber is much more expensive than sawn, simply because it takes time to plane up the sawn timber. There are therefore big savings to be made by planing up your own timber for all your garden woodworking projects.

The planer consists of an electric motor that drives a circular drum in which are set two blades. When the motor is activated, the drum spins at enormous speed, and as the operator pushes the planer along the sawn timber the blades take off thousands of fine wood shavings, thereby producing a smooth 'planed' piece of timber. The straight blades in the drum can be exchanged for blades with a 'wavy' edge. If you intend to make decking, this is an ideal accessory for producing anti-slip grooves in the surface. The Bosch planer has an accessory that allows the plane to cut rebates and angles in timber. A 'V' guide is fitted in the sole plate which allows for very rapid chamfering of all sharp edges.

Of all the tools I recommend, this is the one that requires especially careful handling. With a cutter blade rotating at 22,000 revolutions per minute there is no room for mistakes, and it is essential that the timber to be planed is fixed firmly to the workbench. When you have learned to use it, however, you will be able to buy the roughest-looking timber for a fraction of the cost of the ready-planed version and prepare it yourself, and as you progress you will begin to appreciate just how many other DIY jobs now come within your scope.

Hand-held planer
Of all the tools you use, this is the one that requires especially careful handling.

TIMBER

TODAY WE ARE ONLY TOO AWARE OF THE DEPLETING TIMBER STOCKS IN THE WORLD. MOST OF THE TIMBERS USED IN THE BRITISH ISLES ARE IMPORTED FROM FINLAND, NORWAY AND SWEDEN – SO HOW DO THESE COUNTRIES MANAGE THEIR FORESTS? DO THEY FELL EVERY TREE IN SIGHT, OR IS THERE A CLEAR POLICY OF TIMBER REGENERATION? IN FACT, THE SCANDINAVIAN COUNTRIES HAVE PRACTISED SUSTAINABLE FORESTRY FOR OVER 200 YEARS, AND PLANT MORE TREES THAN THEY CUT. TAKING JUST SWEDEN AND FINLAND, THIS AMOUNTS TO A CULTIVATED FOREST AREA TWICE THE LAND MASS OF THE ENTIRE BRITISH ISLES.

Visit any good timber or builder's merchant and they should be able to offer you a variety of 'Nordic' timbers. There will be stocks of red pine and spruce: the latter, derived from the species we know as the Christmas tree, is a lighter colour and is sometimes called 'whitewood', while the Scots pine produces 'redwood', sometimes simply called 'red'.

Nordic red is really good to saw, plane and shape, so for projects that require this – such as the box bench (p88) – I would choose this wood. Whitewood is usually cheaper and is a little more difficult to work, so you will need to sharpen all your tools before you start. It is used to make the battens for the trellises (p42), and tongue and grooved floorboards (see below). As it is very good

A KNOTTY PROBLEM

Trees have branches, and knots form where these leave the trunk. I am not suggesting that someone should start to breed branchless trees, far from it, however, when dealing with relatively small sections of timber, such as roofing batten, a knot in the wrong place means that a 7ft (2m) batten can, quite literally, fall in half. You should look at the wood carefully and wherever possible select knot free lengths for the vertical pieces, particularly for the trellises (p20, 26 and 42). However, the majority of horizontal pieces on the trellises are short, so do not present so much of a problem.

at shedding water, it is also useful for items that will be in very damp situations. Planter box bases, for instance, can be constructed out of tongue and groove floorboards, which last extremely well.

Nordic red pine and spruce are ideal for making all the projects in this book.

BATTENS

Roofing battens can be bought in bundles from a good builder's merchant or timber yard. I use a great many roof battens in my garden projects: they are inexpensive and ideal for trellis work. They also come in three different sizes, so there is plenty of choice. For example, the trellis in the archway project (p52) uses the smallest section batten available.

TONGUE AND GROOVE FLOORBOARDS

These are, in fact, standard flooring boards – so easily available at your builder's merchant or timber yard and easy to use. The boards fit together like a jigsaw and are useful for planking in an area, such as the base of the planting trough (p32) or floor of the tool store (p82). When 'locked' together, the boards form a 'wooden wall' of natural strength.

A tongue or groove should only be cut off when it is on the outer edge of an item, for example the front and back of the potting bench (p64). In this situation, there is no advantage to leaving them in place – in fact, they would just look ugly.

With tongue and groove boards, the width of the tongue is not important: it is the 'covering' (width of the board without the tongue) that matters; unless otherwise stated, this is the measurement given in the cutting lists for the projects.

SHIPLAP

The wood used to make the roof in the bird table (p76) is known as shiplap and is used for cladding sheds. It is pre-shaped and fits together in such a way that it prevents water getting between the boards. Instead, the water runs from one interlocked board to the next and eventually off the shed or bird table.

CHOOSING TIMBER

When you visit the timber merchant, remember to take along the cutting list for the project you wish to make. Late morning is a good time to go, when all the professionals have got their supplies for the day, as you will get better service.

The timber merchant should be able to offer you several different grades of timber. Do not buy wood that has been stored in the open – some timber that is stacked inside may actually have been stored outside, so check to see that it is dry. Nordic timber is kiln-dried before export, so not only is the quality first rate but it should be dry, too.

Check the timber for knots (see box), and pull planks from the stack and 'eye' them lengthways, rejecting any that are twisted.

Sawn or Planed?

Most builder's merchants stock both sawn and planed timber. Sawn timber is supplied straight off the saw and is usually fairly tough – ideal for trellises, sheds and so on, but not so comfortable to sit on! It can, of course, be planed up at home, but unless you have an electric-powered hand planer (see p13) this will be a lot of work. However, some sawn boards are smoother than others, so keep your eyes open for a bargain.

Planed timber is planed on all four surfaces and is known as PSE – planed square edge. It is more expensive than sawn timber but can save you a lot of time. Also, it allows you to make a start on your project as soon as you get the wood home.

Tongue and groove floorboards and shiplap come ready planed, but do select carefully as some are of much better quality than others.

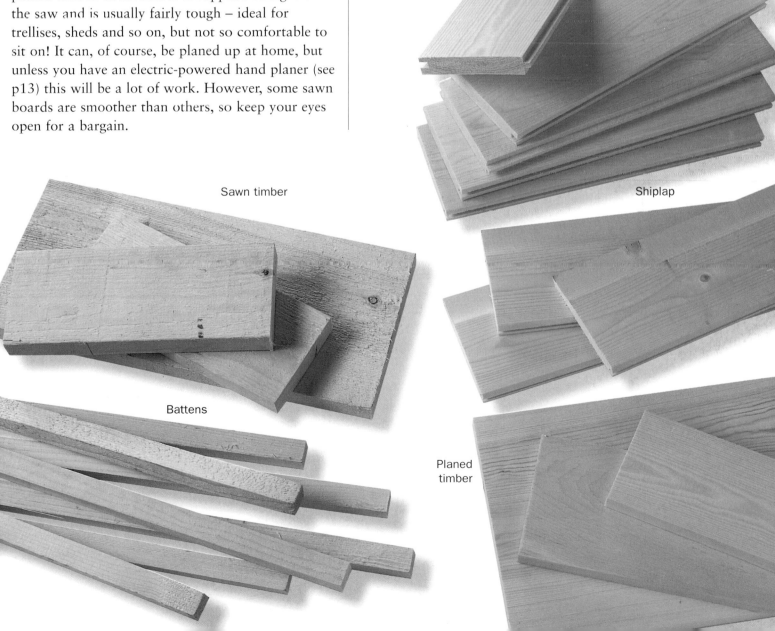

Tongue and groove floorboards

Sawn timber

Shiplap

Battens

Planed timber

SUNDRIES

THERE ARE VARIOUS ITEMS THAT ARE NEEDED TO
ASSEMBLE THE PROJECTS OR PROVIDE THE FINISHING
TOUCHES. THESE ARE LISTED BELOW.

GLUES

The industrial chemist has played a large part in the
development of woodworking techniques by
introducing glues that are actually stronger than the
timber they stick. In the correct temperatures, these
wood glues are able to cure (dry) in under two
hours. For outdoor items it is important to buy a
glue that is also water-resistant. This is ideal for
garden furniture or any other job where the wood
will not be immersed in water. Water-resistant glues
are clearly labelled as such. The widely available
Extrarez is one of my favourites.

SUPASCREWS

In recent years screw makers have changed the
design of the screw: the thread is far coarser and it is
now twin threaded, and the screw points are very
sharp. Screws are now zinc-plated, which prevents
rust – a big bonus for all garden woodwork.

The very latest innovation is a dry lubricant,
rolled into the screw during manufacture. Previously
a 'tight' screw had to be taken out and the threads
rubbed with candle wax. Now it is all done for you
before you purchase the screws, making the task of
screw driving so very much more pleasant.

Quite literally there are dozens of screw sizes
available. Remember the screw is not only sold by
its length but also by its gauge. For almost all our
purposes a number 8 gauge is ideal.

SCREW EYES

A screw eye has a threaded screw shaft at one end
and a complete loop eye at the other. Fitted into a
rawlplug, screw eyes can be used for attaching
trellises to a garden or house wall.

TERRY CLIPS

These bright chrome clips are perfect for holding
tool handles, and keeping things tidy and in their
place. The clips are spring steel and have a single
screw fixing at the back. They are available in a
range of sizes.

HINGES

Self-recessing hinges are ideal, as you do not need to
cut a recess in the timber first – simply position the
hinge and screw it in place.

HANDLES

It helps to have a handle on an item such as the box
bench (see p88). Handles are available in a variety of
shapes and sizes; the 'forged' type look most
appropriate on country style furniture like this bench.

WHEELS AND AXLES

Trolley wheels and axle rods can be purchased at
DIY stores, and this is best done before you start
work on the project itself to make sure you are
working to the correct size. The wheels are held in
place by a clever device called a spring clip, which
simply pushes on to the end of the axle, preventing
the wheel from coming off.

FELT NAILS

Felt nails are zinc-plated and have a large flat head
which holds the felt firmly to the roof beneath. They
are available in a variety of sizes.

PACKAGING AND MASKING TAPES

These tapes are very useful for holding light pieces
of wood together while the glue is drying. Modern
glues do not need huge amounts of pressure when
bonding small timber sections, and packaging or
masking tape is a handy alternative to clamps.

TEMPLATES

Some of the designs in this book, for example
the box bench (p88), have a curve or other
shape cut into the wood for a more elegant
finish. One of the simplest methods of
transferring a shape from the construction
diagram is to make a full-size template or
pattern from stiff card – a section of a
cardboard box will do. Once you have drawn the
shape on the card, cut it out and place it in
position on the wood. Draw around the outline
with a pencil and then cut out the wood using a
jigsaw or coping saw.

TECHNIQUES

IN WOODWORKING MOST OF THE TECHNIQUES ARE ABOUT FIXING SECTIONS OF TIMBER TOGETHER. IN TRADITIONAL WOODWORKING BOOKS THIS WOULD MEAN MAKING JOINTS, WHICH CAN BE FIDDLY AND TIME-CONSUMING. APART FROM ONE JOINT (SEE P63) ALL THE PROJECTS IN THIS BOOK ARE SCREWED AND GLUED TOGETHER. THIS MEANS THAT ALL YOU HAVE TO BE CAPABLE OF IS: MEASURING AND CUTTING TIMBER, DRILLING A HOLE TO TAKE A SCREW, DRIVING SCREWS INTO TIMBER, GLUING, AND USING SANDPAPER.

MEASURING AND CUTTING

This is a job for the expanding rule, a pencil, a carpenter's square (or a Jetcut saw, see p9), and a saw. If there is more than one piece of the same size, for example four legs, mark them together so that you are assured of a uniform length.

Once it is marked, hold the timber firmly on the workbench with one hand and start cutting it to length with the other. The mistake that beginners often make at this stage is to let the saw blade tilt and so under-cut the bottom edge of the wood, making an angled rather than a flat end. To avoid this, try to keep the blade at 90 degrees to the surface of the wood you are cutting down. The fine-toothed saw is always the best for this operation. If your lengths of wood are very long then get an assistant to hold the end being cut off to avoid producing an ugly splintered edge.

BORING HOLES

If you drive a nail or screw into a piece of wood without first boring a hole to accommodate it, there is a real possibility that you will split the wood. Screw Sinks (see p10) are ideal for making a pilot hole as they will both bore a hole and cut a recess for the screw head to lie flush with the surface of the wood. Alternatively, you can use a countersink to make a recess. Countersinking the screw heads is vital to avoid catching fingers, legs and clothes on them when using the finished project.

DRIVING SCREWS

Just about everybody I know has, at some time, experienced difficulties getting screws into timber. First bore the correct size hole (see above).

Old-fashioned slot-head screws are difficult to drive in, especially if you have not got the correct size screwdriver as this is liable to slip off when under pressure and mark the wood you have spent so many hours on. When a slot-head screwdriver blade gets worn, it no longer grips the screw, so it needs sharpening with a file until it fits firmly again. However, the majority of screwdrivers sold today are of the Philips or Posidriv pattern to fit crosshead screws. Driving in a crosshead screw in is far simpler. For a start, the screwdriver end is held more firmly in the screw so there is far less tendency for it to slip out as you rotate the screwdriver. Another great advantage is that there is far less chance of the screw head disintegrating as can happen with the old, slot-pattern type.

It is not just the design of the screwdriver blade that has changed. Stanley's Magnum screwdrivers have handles that are ergonomically correct and made of plastic in two parts so they are far more comfortable to grip and, even when your hands get hot, there is far less chance of slipping.

It is worth mentioning that, should you get really keen on woodwork, a battery-powered screwdriver is a good investment and does the job so much faster than the traditional method (see p12).

GLUING

The reason for using glue and screws in each joint is simply that a glued joint has greater strength and rigidity than one that is only screwed. Always use both methods of fixing timber together. When gluing, make sure that the timber does not slip after you have clasped it together – the glue will be slippery until it sets.

SANDPAPERING

When sandpapering by hand, use a cork block and wrap the sandpaper around it. Do not be tempted to use a very coarse grade of paper as it will score the wood – medium to fine grade is ideal. The cork block will assist you in giving the surface an all-over pressure and prevents 'digging in'.

If you use an orbital random sander, you will be amazed at how long one sheet of sandpaper lasts. These machines do a far better job than is possible by hand, and achieve a superb finish very quickly.

FINISHING OFF

IT IS OFTEN SAID THAT A BEAUTIFUL ITEM CAN BE SPOILED IN THE FINISHING PROCESS, SO CARE AT THIS STAGE IS WELL-ADVISED. DEPENDING ON WHERE IT IS BEING USED, TIMBER HAS A CERTAIN AMOUNT OF ROT-RESISTANCE IN ITS NATURAL STATE. FOR EXAMPLE, A TRELLIS FIXED TO A WALL OR FENCE WILL BE IN THE PERFECT PLACE TO DRY OFF AFTER A SHOWER, WHILE THE BOTTOM OF A WOODEN PLANTER BOX WILL BE IN CONTACT WITH DAMP SOIL THROUGHOUT ITS LIFE, AND SO IS MUCH MORE LIABLE TO ROT.

CHOOSING WOOD-CARE PRODUCTS

Most softwoods need treating with some sort of wood-care product, and if this is done at the outset then re-coating need only take place every four years. Not only do modern treatments enable you to protect the wood, but they also allow you to choose a colour to fit in with your garden colour scheme.

There is a wide choice of wood stains, which offer varying degrees of protection. I use Sadolin, which is available in a range of colours and finishes, providing excellent weather protection and long lasting beauty. It is possible to choose stains that will be touch dry in 1–2 hours (Sadolin rapid). If you have an item, such as an obelisk, that needs treating but already has an established plant on it, then use a water-based product (Sadolin Scenic Colours) as it will be less harmful to the plant.

For certain items, it is worth considering the Scandinavian method of preserving wood: they usually use sawn boards, which are much rougher than planed timber so the preservative 'keys' into the surface and holds there much more easily than it does on a planed surface. However, although this is ideal for some garden structures it may not be so comfortable for chairs and benches!

CHOOSING BRUSHES

When applying wood-care products, it is important to use a good-quality brush. Cheap brushes lose their hairs on your work and do not apply the stain as effectively. With garden furniture there are lots of battens and spars, so applying stain can be quite fiddly. I have two brushes, large and small, the latter for brushing away or removing any excess stain from the edges of the wood – nothing looks worse

than thick, dripping deposits of stain on the underside of the item.

USING WOOD-CARE PRODUCTS

The manufacturers of wood-care products have spent many years experimenting with the best ways to finish off wood items. So, although it sounds obvious, it is important to read the instructions on the tin of your chosen product before you start.

If you are using water-based wood stains, the bare or undercoated wood needs to be slightly damp. You can wet it by wiping over the surface with a moistened lint-free cloth. This will aid the application of the stain and give the best possible finish but is not necessary when using a traditional solvent-based product.

Brush the stain well into the grain, then finish off with strokes in the direction of the grain, along a complete brush length. Apply liberally and lay off evenly: with garden furniture there are usually spars and rails, so it is important to watch out for any uneven application. After application the surface may have a slight texture. This is caused by the wood grain being 'raised' because wood swells when it gets damp or wet. For the best results, lightly rub over with sandpaper between the second and third coat to get rid of this texture, but do not break the surface of the dried film.

One of the many benefits of the water-based wood stains is that they have a very low odour, so it is possible to work in the garage.

With quick-drying wood stains, cleaning brushes is simplicity itself – just wash them out with water. With the traditional finishes use white spirit.

MAINTENANCE

In the springtime, when we are looking forward to the prospect of long warm days, it is worth checking benches, tables and so on, to see that they look their best for the summer. Sandpaper very lightly over the whole surface and then wash down with a liquid detergent and warm water, rinse off and wipe dry. Check the surface for damage, and touch in any bare areas to match the surrounding colour. In garden benches or tables the favourite spot for damp and algae is the bottom of the legs. Pay special attention to endgrain areas to prevent ingress of water.

THE PROJECTS

OBELISK

There are a variety of climbing plants that love structures to grow up in the garden: sweet peas and clematis are just two of the most popular. This obelisk can be positioned anywhere in the garden and its height adds an extra dimension.

Using the basic design here it is possible to build taller obelisks if you wish, bearing in mind that such high structures, especially when covered with climbing plants, need to anchored well into the ground, particularly if your garden is in a windy location.

Difficulty Rating

Dimensions

Height	74in (1880mm)
Width	24in (610mm)
Depth	24in (610mm)

Design tip

The decoration on the top is a matter of choice. I like spikes, but you can use balls. If you want a ball, I suggest that you buy one as they are very difficult to make. Use roofing batten (see p14) for the trellis.

Tools

Pencil, expanding rule, carpenter's square, protractor (for angles), clamps, Jetcut tenon saw, surform tool or small plane, drill, drill bits and countersink, bradawl, screwdriver.

Sundries

Zinc-plated supascrews (1¹/₂in/38mm No. 8), glue, packaging tape, wood-care product, metal posts (optional).

Cutting List

Legs	4	66 x 2 x 2in (1676 x 50 x 50mm)
Bottom tie bars	4	23¼ x 2 x 1in (590 x 50 x 25mm)
Top tie bars	4	4½ x 2 x 1in (114 x 50 x 25mm)
Capping piece	1	5¼ x 5¼ x 1in (133 x 133 x 25mm)
Spike	1	8½ x 2 x 2in (216 x 50 x 50mm)
Dowel rod	1	8 x ¾in (203 x 19mm) diameter
Trellis batten		540 x 1 x ¾in (13716 x 25 x 19mm)

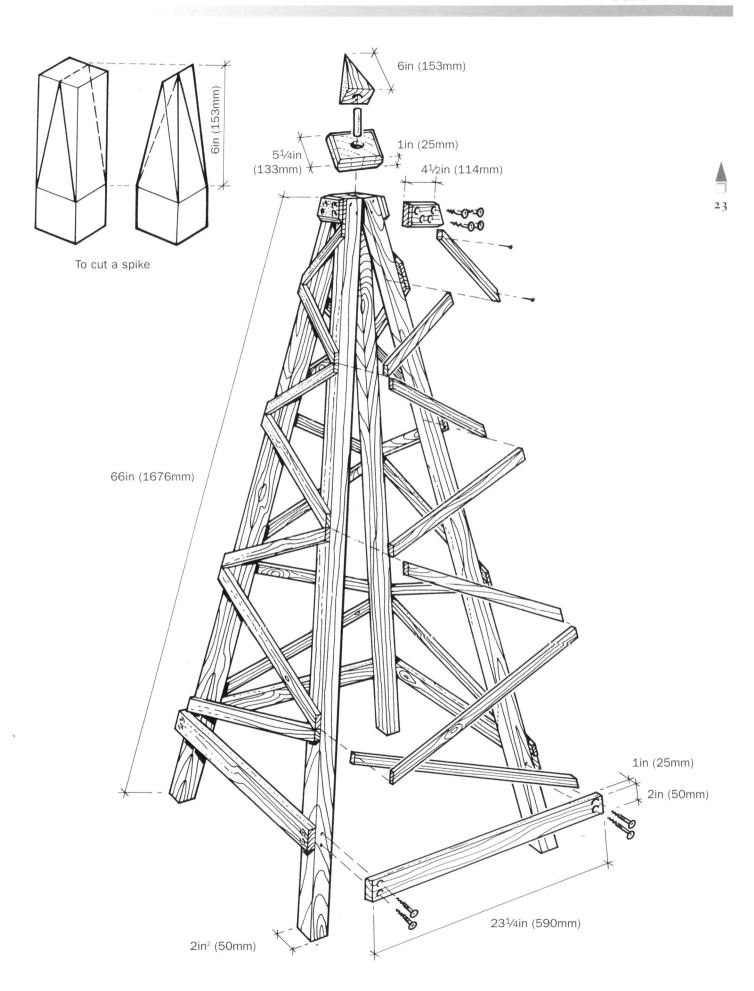

To cut a spike

6in (153mm)

6in (153mm)

5¼in (133mm)

1in (25mm)

4½in (114mm)

66in (1676mm)

1in (25mm)

2in (50mm)

23¼in (590mm)

2in² (50mm)

Construction
MAIN STRUCTURE

1 The main structure consists of four equal lengths of timber for the legs. Fasten these together with a clamp or packaging tape. Pencil a line 4in (100mm) up from the bottom. Using a carpenter's square, draw the line across all four legs.

2 Separate the legs again and project the pencilled line around all four sides of all four pieces.

3 From the drawing, prepare the four tie bars for the bottom of the obelisk and the four for the top. Note the angle that it is necessary to mark and cut on the end of each batten. The Jetcut saw is perfect for this task.

4 Prepare the tie bars for fixing to the uprights by boring two holes in the ends of each. The holes are best countersunk after they are bored, to allow the screw heads to lie flush with the surface of the timber.

5 Assemble the first side of the obelisk. The best way to do this is to envisage it as making a large triangle in wood. The two uprights are laid out on a flat surface in a triangular shape. Position the long tie bar at the base of the uprights and the shorter tie bar at the top. Be prepared to jiggle the pieces around until they fit. Align the lower side of the long tie bar with the pencilled lines made earlier on the bottoms of the legs (steps 1 and 2). It is helpful to have an extra spare pair of hands to help hold things together at this point. Once you are satisfied that everything is in the right place, glue and screw on the top and bottom tie bars.

6 Forming the second triangle is simpler as you can lie the bits for it over the top of the first triangle, using it as a template. This way you can be sure you are getting the second side's angles accurate.

7 Now you have formed two triangles of the obelisk, it remains for you to screw the remaining tie bars in place. You cannot do this job alone, so with an assistant holding both triangles, and working on a flat surface, glue and screw on first the final two long bottom tie bars and next the two smaller tie bars. You should have the framework of the obelisk.

TRELLIS AND SPIKE

1 The fill-in battens need to be cut to length and screwed to the obelisk. Four on each side will be sufficient, but you can choose how many you wish. Measure the battens against the obelisk to get the correct length. As you are using small-section batten, drill pilot screw holes to avoid splitting the wood.

2 Make the top of the obelisk by drilling a hole in the middle of the capping piece to accept a dowel rod. The capping piece is screwed on to the battens; normally two screws are quite sufficient. If you wish to bevel the capping piece as shown below, cut the piece bigger – 6¹/2in (164mm) square should be adequate to allow for bevelling.

3 With a pencil, mark the shape of the spike on to one side of a piece of timber of the same dimensions as the legs (with luck you will have an offcut). Make sure the piece is over length so that you have something to hold on to while cutting the end. Using a tenon saw, and with the timber firmly clamped down or in a vice, cut down two sides to form half of the spike. Now, and only at this stage, you can pencil in the other two sides, then cut them down in the same way. Once this is done, use a surform tool to remove the saw marks. Cut off the surplus length then drill a hole in the base to take a short length of dowel rod. Glue one end of the dowel rod into the spike and the other end into the top of the obelisk.

FINISHING

Use a wood-care product as described on p18. If the obelisk is to be sited in an exposed position then it is worth considering the purchase of metal posts, consisting of a socket at one end and a long steel spike at the other. These are readily available at DIY stores. The spike is driven into the ground and the wooden leg of the obelisk is fitted into the socket. Holes in the socket allow screws to be driven into the wood thus securing it to the post. Two metal sockets should be sufficient to hold the obelisk securely in the ground.

VERSAILLES TUB
WITH OBELISK TOP

One of the basic methods of joining timbers together has always been the mortice and tenon joint. This joint, however, is quite difficult for a novice to master, and also requires access to a number of rather specialized tools. Therefore, the challenge for me was to design a box structure that was free from traditional joints, but still had sufficient strength to do the job. The obelisk top requires a degree of patience to build well; you also need a jig to assemble it on – but more of that later.

Difficulty Rating

PLANTER 🔫 🔫

OBELISK TOP 🔫 🔫 🔫 🔫

Design tip
The plywood panels are exterior-grade waterproof and boil (W.P.B), essential for this hardworking outdoor item.

Tools
Pencil, expanding rule, Stanley knife, protractor (for marking angles), clamps, Jetcut panel saw, Jetcut tenon saw, plane or surform tool, drill, drill bits and countersink, bradawl, hammer, screwdriver.

Sundries
Zinc-plated supascrews (1¾in/ 44mm No. 8 for planter, 1¼in/ 32mm No. 8 for obelisk), glue, wood-care product.

Cutting List

PLANTER BOX

Legs	4	19 x 2 x 2in (483 x 50 x 50mm)
Plywood panels	4	16 x 16 x ¾in (406 x 406 x 19mm)
Leg and side battens		
verticals	8	16¾ x ¾ x ¾in (425 x 19 x 19mm)
top and bottom	8	14¼ x ¾ x ¾in (362 x 19 x 19mm)
Base T&G board (covering is 4½in/114mm per board)	5	18 x 4½ x ⅞in (457 x 114 x 22mm)
Top edge	4	22¼ x 3½ x ⅞in (565 x 90 x 22mm)
Obelisk stop blocks	4	3 x ⅞ x ⅞in (76 x 22 x 22mm)

OBELISK TOP

Legs	4	60¼ x 1 x 1in (1530 x 25 x 25mm)
Bottom cross piece battens	2	17 x 1 x 1in (431 x 25 x 25mm)
Bottom cross piece battens	2	15 x 1 x 1in (381 x 25 x 25mm)
Top cross piece battens	2	3½ x 1 x 1in (89 x 25 x 25mm)
Top cross piece battens	2	2 x 1 x 1in (50 x 25 x 25mm)
Spike top	1	6½ x 2 x 2in (165 x 50 x 50mm)
Dowel rod	1	¼in (6mm) diameter
Trellis lathe		480 x 1 x ¼in (12192 x 25 x 6mm)

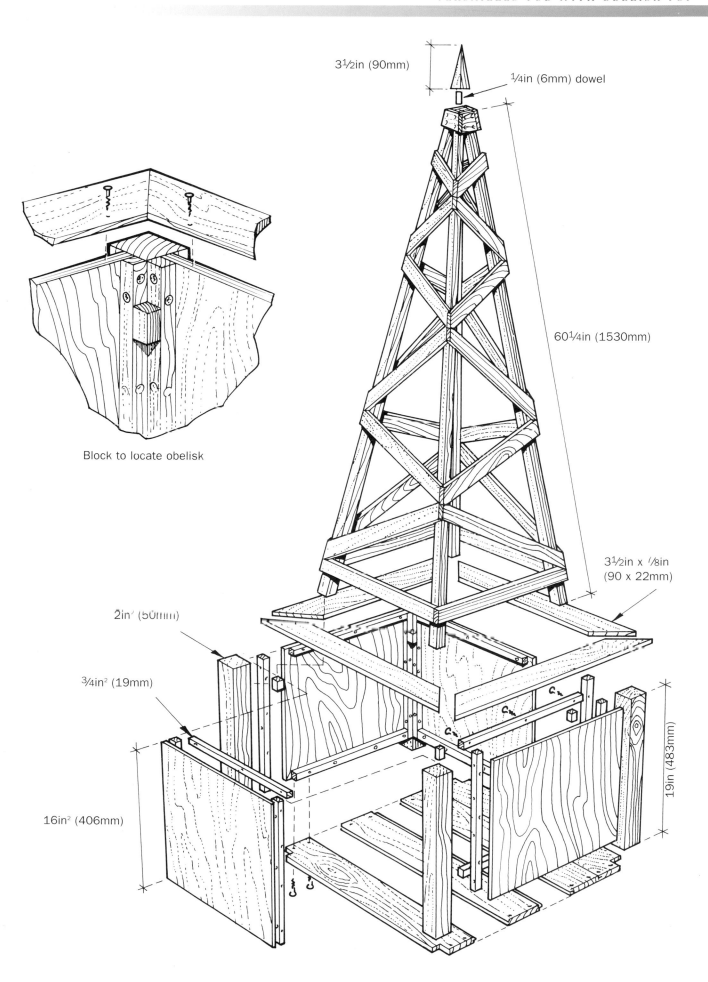

3½in (90mm)

¼in (6mm) dowel

60¼in (1530mm)

3½in x ⅞in
(90 x 22mm)

Block to locate obelisk

2in² (50mm)

¾in² (19mm)

16in² (406mm)

19in (483mm)

Dimensions of box
Height   20in (508mm)
Width   22in (559mm)

Dimensions of obelisk
Height   66in (1676mm)
Width   17in (432mm)

Construction
PLANTER BOX

1 Cut to length the four legs of the box. Fix them together with tape, and pencil in a line 4in (100mm) up from the bottom. This marks the lower position of the internal battens; their tops should be flush with the tops of the legs. The lower section of the leg forms the foot of the planter.

2 You now need eight battens, all cut to identical length. These are then screwed on to the two inside faces of each of the legs, with their tops flush with the leg tops (see inset diagram). Use both glue and screws to hold the battens in position.

3 The sides are made with exterior-grade plywood. The glue used in this ply is unaffected by damp and wet. Cut to size four identical pieces of this plywood then bore and countersink holes to take screws.

4 The plywood panels are now glued and screwed to the battens (see diagram). It is important to keep the top of the panel flush with the top of the leg. Once all four panels are screwed in place a bottomless box is formed.

5 In order to make a bottom, battens are screwed to the lower edges of each of the plywood sides. It is important

that at least four screws per batten are used as, ultimately, the whole weight of the soil or potting compost that fills the tub will rest on these battens.

6 The base is made from standard tongue and groove flooring boards. You will have to cut off the tongue of one of the outer edge boards and the groove on the other outer edge board to keep things tidy. Then, because the legs protrude into the inner corners of the box, you have to cut out two small squares in each of these two end boards to fit them around the legs. Make pencil marks of the shapes of the pieces you are cutting off and remove them with a tenon saw.

7 Fitting the boards requires a little know how. Assemble all the boards, fitting tongues and grooves together. Turn the box upside down. As you push the assembled boards into place they will arch in the middle, however, press down lightly in the middle and all the tongues and grooves will snap together. If this does not happen then trim a little bit more from the cut-outs around the legs, and try again.

8 Screw the base very well to the battens around the bottom edges. Now bore holes at random to allow for drainage; these holes need to be fairly large – at least ½in (12mm).

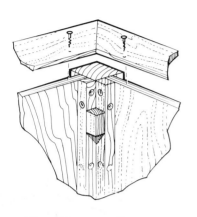

9 Now turn your attention to the top of the box which wants strips of timber to cap it off. Although it is not essential, these look really very nice when cut to 45 degree mitres at the corners. If you decide that you are confident enough to have a go, then mark out a 45 degree line and use a tenon saw to cut carefully along the line. Repeat for the next piece of timber until all ends have 45 degree cuts. It sounds simple, but aligning them all is not so easy.

The alternative is to retain straight edges on the top boards and simply butt them up.

Before you attach the top of box edges to the legs (see diagram) you need to screw the upper battens in place around the top edges of the box. This process is really a repeat of the job you did for the base (step 5), only, in this case, they will not be carrying any weight so don't need so many screws.

OBELISK TOP

You may have already built the large, free-standing obelisk (p20), and, having found that fairly straightforward, decided to make this one using the same method; well it is not quite so simple. The timber is far more delicate and a jig is required to hold the pieces together while the glue sets.

1 Make a start by sketching a full-size drawing of one side of the obelisk on a piece of plywood. This will be the basis of a jig on which to position and hold the sides of the obelisk during construction; without this it is a real problem to glue, screw and hold all the bits together. Along the pencil lines screw some small blocks of wood – 2in (50mm) offcuts will be fine. The purpose of the blocks is to keep the uprights and cross pieces in place while the glue dries.

2 Place the main uprights in the jig and carefully drill pilot holes in the cross pieces. Because the sections of the timber are fairly delicate it is best to drill and countersink all the holes. It is also very important to glue all the joints together, the glue giving great rigidity to the structure.

Make up two sides of the obelisk in this way.

3 Once the glue is fully cured (dried) the two frames are ready for the bottom cross piece battens to be glued and screwed in place. You need an assistant to hold the ready-glued frames while the battens are being attached.

4 The trellis work can be attached when the glue is cured. Once again drill all screw holes, otherwise there is a tendency for small battening to split when the screws are driven in. Before you finally fix all the parts of the trellis in place carry out a fit check: to fix the obelisk top into the planter it is necessary to glue four small blocks on to the corner battens, inside the planter (see diagram). These form a base for the feet of the obelisk. Sit the obelisk top on these and make sure it is snug, then fix the remaining trellis sections in place.

5 A spiked top is now made. This is purely a matter of choice; you can fit a ball top if you wish. The spike is best fashioned from a leftover length of timber (see p25, trellis and spike, step 3).

FINISHING
Use a wood-care product as described on p18.

TROUGH WITH TRELLIS

No matter whether you live in the town or the country, have a big garden or a small patio, a paved back yard or a tiny balcony, this planter will fit. The trough is suitable for extending or shortening so you can alter its size for any space you have.

This is a sturdy design with substantial timbers that will last for years, with just a little maintenance. The curved sides give elegance to the trough, and prevent it looking boxy: the pieces cut out to make the curves serve as handles, so there is little waste.

Difficulty Rating

Dimensions

Height	39¼in (997mm)
Width	35in (890mm)
Depth	10¾in (273mm)

Design Tip

Cutting the curves in the trough sides is not difficult if you have the right tools. It is a quick, simple task with an electric jigsaw, but a coping saw will also do the job very efficiently – although obviously a lot slower.

Tools

Pencil, expanding rule, carpenter's square, clamp, Jetcut panel saw, coping saw or jigsaw, surform tool, drill, drill bits and countersink, screwdriver.

Sundries

Zinc-plated supascrews (1½in/38mm No. 8), sandpaper, glue, wood-care product.

Cutting List

Sides	2	32 x 8 x ⅞in (813 x 203 x 22mm)
Ends	2	10⅝ x 8 x ⅞in (270 x 203 x 22mm)
Base T&G board	2	32 x 5½ x ¾in (813 x 140 x 19mm)
Feet	2	13½ x 2¾ x ⅞in (343 x 70 x 22mm)
Handles	2	10⅝ x (270mm)
Battens	7	32 x 1 x ¾in (813 x 25 x 19mm)

Construction

Trough

1 Taking the plank of wood to be used for the trough, mark out the lengths needed for the two sides and two ends, and then using a carpenter's square, make a pencil line right across the board showing where to cut. Cut both sides to length and then the ends.

2 Get an assistant to help you mark out the curves on the front and back of the trough. Using a thin lathe of timber,

bend it to form the desired curve and while you hold the lathe in place, get your assistant to pencil in the shape.

3 Clamp the timber firmly and then, holding the coping saw handle with both hands, start sawing along the curved pencil line. Do not be tempted to force the saw: it is a good idea to have a spare pack of blades, in case of breakages! Remove the saw cut marks from the curves using a surform tool or sandpaper.

4 Using the pieces of curved timber removed from the front and back of the trough, cut lengths to form the end handles. Drill holes through the top of the end pieces and screw both handles into place.

5 Next attach the end pieces on to the front and back pieces: pencil in the positions of all the screw holes, use a small drill bit to bore them through, and then use a countersink to open up the hole so that the head of each

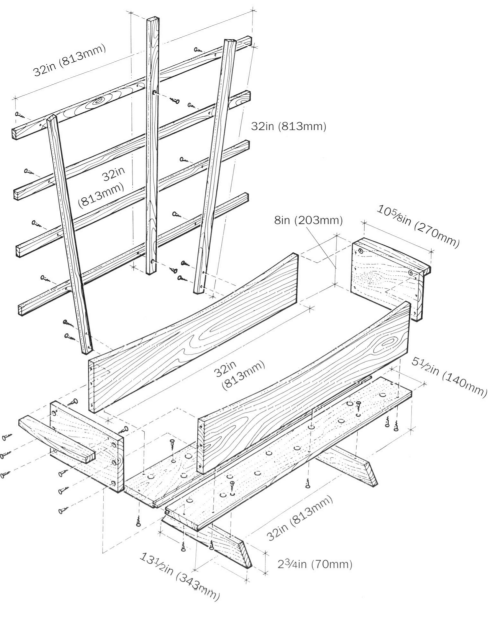

32in (813mm)

32in (813mm)

32in (813mm)

32in (813mm)

8in (203mm)

10⅝in (270mm)

32in (813mm)

5½in (140mm)

32in (813mm)

13½in (343mm)

2¾in (70mm)

screw fits flush with the surface of the timber. Glue and screw in place and then check that the trough corners are square.

6 The base is formed by using two lengths of tongue and groove floor board. Before you fit them together, cut the tongue off one board, and the groove off the other. Drill the boards to take the screws that will hold the base in place, also drill two holes through each end of the base to take the feet and make a random

series of holes for drainage. Now screw the base on to the box.

7 Holding the timber carefully and using a Jetcut saw, cut a 30 degree angle on the ends of both the feet. Turn the box on its side, push screws through the bottom holes and attach the feet.

TRELLIS

1 Position the horizontal battens on your workbench and lay the verticals on top of them. Note that the central vertical spar is

not attached to the back of the trough. You can do the laying-out by eye but measuring everything will be more accurate.

2 Put a spot of glue beneath each joint and, after boring the holes in the battens, screw everything together. Then screw the trellis to the back of the plant trough.

FINISHING

Use a wood-care product as described on p18.

ÉTAGÈRE

Nurturing growing plants and watching as they mature to flowering size is one of the most satisfying things about gardening. However, once the plant is in flower you can increase your enjoyment even more by placing it where it can be seen to best advantage and will add colour and beauty to its surroundings.

The shape and shelving of this étagère make it a particularly good stand on which to display plants with spectacular hanging flowers, such as fuchsias, so that you can appreciate the blooms more easily. Mix these with trailing foliage plants, like ivies, and contrast both with a few taller, more upright pot plants, such as pelargoniums, to create a really eyecatching and balanced display. If you are really keen, you can build two étagères and place them back to back, forming an all-round, circular stand.

Making the étagère requires attention to detail, as angles always add to the complexity of a woodworking task. Determined to have a go? Follow the instructions step by step and study the diagram carefully, and the result will be a superb garden feature that will show off your treasured plants to perfection.

Difficulty Rating 🪛 🪛 🪛

Dimensions

Height	45$^1/_2$in (1155mm)
Width	44$^1/_2$in (1130mm)
Depth	22in (559mm)

Design Tip

The étagère is not the simplest stand to make due to the many angles that have to be cut on the legs and bracing bars and the curved shelves that need to be shaped using a jigsaw. Make a careful study of the diagram to get a good mental picture of where all the pieces should go.

Cutting List

FRAMEWORK

Back legs	2	45 x 3$^3/_4$ x $^7/_8$in (1143 x 95 x 22mm)
Front leg	1	45 x 3$^3/_4$ x $^7/_8$in (1143 x 95 x 22mm)
Bottom back rail	1	45 x 3$^3/_4$ x $^7/_8$in (1143 x 95 x 22mm)
Middle back rail	1	31 x 3$^3/_4$ x $^7/_8$in (788 x 95 x 22mm)
Top back rail	1	12 x 3$^3/_4$ x $^7/_8$in (305 x 95 x 22mm)
Bracing bars (bottom shelf)	2	20$^1/_4$ x 3$^3/_4$ x $^7/_8$in (514 x 95 x 22mm)
Bracing bars (middle shelf)	2	13 x 3$^3/_4$ x $^7/_8$in (330 x 95 x 22mm)

BOTTOM SHELF

	1	44$^3/_4$ x 2 x $^7/_8$in (1137 x 50 x 22mm)
	1	44$^3/_4$ x 5$^3/_4$ x $^7/_8$in (1137 x 146 x 22mm)
	1	41 x 5$^3/_4$ x $^7/_8$in (1041 x 146 x 22mm)
	2	15 x 4$^1/_4$ x $^7/_8$in (381 x 108 x 22mm)

MIDDLE SHELF

	1	31$^1/_4$ x 5$^3/_4$ x $^7/_8$in (794 x 146 x 22mm)
	2	13$^3/_4$ x 5$^3/_4$ x $^7/_8$in (349 x 146 x 22mm)

TOP SHELF AND BACK

	2	13$^1/_2$ x 5$^1/_2$ x $^7/_8$in (343 x 140 x 22mm)

BATTENS

Bottom shelf	2	21 x 1$^1/_4$ x $^7/_8$in (534 x 31 x 22mm)
Bottom shelf	2	18 x 1$^1/_4$ x $^7/_8$in (457 x 31 x 22mm)
Middle shelf	4	10 x 1$^1/_4$ x $^7/_8$in (254 x 31 x 22mm)

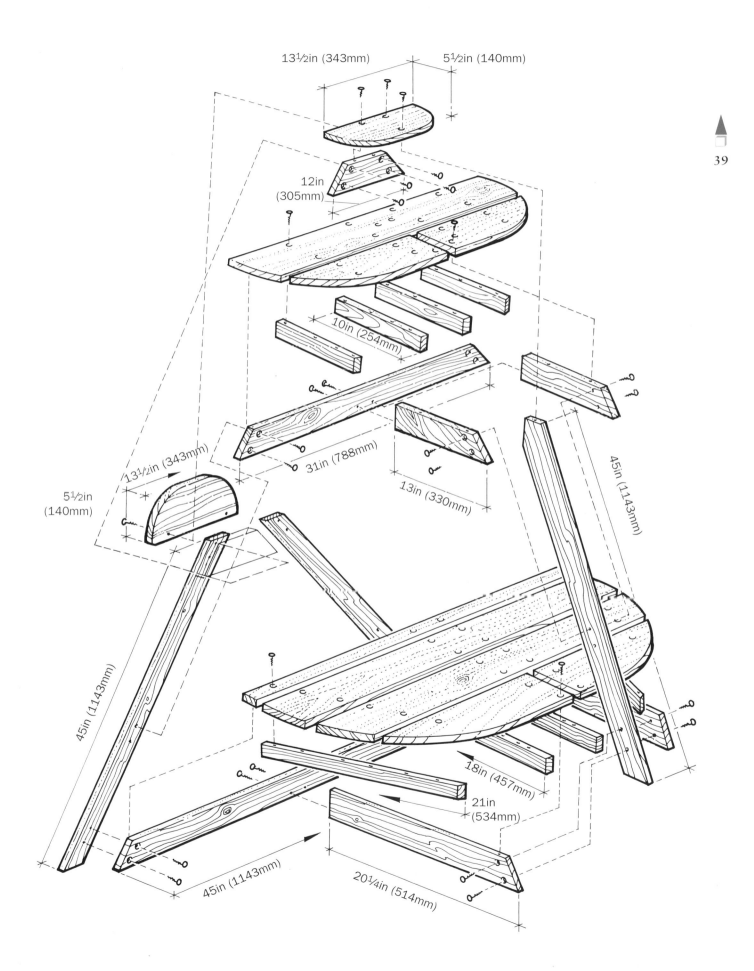

13½in (343mm)

5½in (140mm)

12in (305mm)

13½in (343mm)

5½in (140mm)

10in (254mm)

31in (788mm)

13in (330mm)

45in (1143mm)

45in (1143mm)

18in (457mm)

21in (534mm)

45in (1143mm)

20¼in (514mm)

Tools

Pencil, expanding rule, sliding bevel gauge, protractor, Jigsaw, Jetcut panel saw, surform tool, chisels, drill, drill bits and countersink, screwdriver.

Sundries

Zinc-plated supascrews (1 1/2in/38mm No. 8, 2 1/2in/63mm No. 8 for fixing front leg), glue, wood-care product.

Construction
FRAMEWORK

1 The first job is to construct the large triangular shape that forms the back of the stand.

Lay the pieces of wood out on the ground in the triangular shape and, using a protractor and a sliding bevel gauge, carefully mark off the angles that need to be cut on the bottom of the back legs, to ensure they sit flat on the ground, and on the ends of the bottom rail, which holds the triangle together at the base. Also mark out the small top rail.

From the bottom of the legs measure up 3in (75mm); this gives you the position for the underside of the bottom rail. The top rail should fit snugly with all the angles at the top of the frame.

Before you fix the rails in place, bore and countersink holes in them to take the screws. You need only prepare screw holes in the rails as the screws will not split the legs beneath when the screw is driven home. Use glue as well as screws at all points. It is helpful to use masking tape to hold things together lightly while you are working. You may have to adjust the pieces slightly to get everything to line up, but do not be too anxious if all the edges are not exactly flush, they can always be trimmed up with a surform tool once the glue has dried.

2 Cut the angles on the bottom and top of the front leg. You will need an assistant to hold the leg while you drive two long screws through the top rail and into the front leg from behind. There is room between the converging back legs to bore and countersink two holes for this operation. Don't forget the glue. Once the screws are tightened up it is surprising just how firmly the front leg is now attached to the rear triangle.

3 Once this leg is in place, position the two bracing bars that tie the bottom of the front leg to the bottom back rail and form supports for the shelves. Cut the angles on the front of these bars before fixing them to the bottom back rail and front leg with glue and screws.

4 Repeat step 3 to attach the bracing bars that support the middle shelf. Once this work is complete you have done the hardest part as you have formed the main framework on to which shelves are mounted.

SHELVES

The shelves, battens and bracing bars form a very rigid platform when all is glued and screwed together.

1 I always find it easier to mark out curves using full-sized templates (see p16). Once the templates have been prepared, place them on the timber and pencil in the curved lines. It is not essential to cut the shapes using an electric jigsaw but if you are not used to the non-power equivalent – the coping saw – you will find using a jigsaw far easier and much quicker.

Make sure you clamp the timber down well before starting to cut, and always watch that, as the cut proceeds, you do not slice into the table beneath or the trailing flex of the jigsaw. Once all the shaping is complete remove the saw cuts using a surform tool.

2 Lie all the shelves on a flat surface, spacing them out as if they were fixed on to the framework. On the bottom shelf, mark right across the shelf with a pencil line, indicating the centre of the bracing bars beneath. Now mark in a line for a series of screw holes for the battens that are to be fitted beneath. Marking out needs to be done with great care, otherwise you will have holes in the wrong place. You will always find it an advantage

to assemble the shelves dry (without glue) and see that everything fits nicely together before committing yourself with glue on the surfaces.

3 Repeat this process for the middle shelf.

4 The top shelf is the last to be shaped and fixed. Note that it has no battens and that there is a screw going into the top of the front leg, through the shelf.

FINISHING

Use a good wood-care product as described on p18. If the étagère is kept indoors then the preservative will prevent water-spill marks when the plants are watered; if it is kept outside then preservative is essential to prevent the wood deteriorating.

TRELLISES

The overall method for making all the trellises is identical, however there is a knack to getting each one right. From the variety of designs given, it is best to start with a simple one and the oblong trellis (p44) is the simplest.

With its nice wide splay at the top, the V-shaped fan trellis (p46) is ideal for training honeysuckle. It requires an assistant to help with bending the battens and the end result is a very satisfying and attractive frame. Having tried your hand at bending timber, it is a natural progression to make the stylish curved trellis (p48), which brightens up any wall.

No doubt by the time you get on to making the large fan trellis (p49), you will be very competent at cutting battens and boring holes, and will have acquired the knack of knowing when a screw is going to split the wood, so this is the chance to flex your artistic abilities. The fan trellis looks beautiful in a winter garden, adding colour and interest. Of all the trellises, this is my favourite.

It is quite fun making the obelisk (p50) and far simpler than you might think at first glance. Climbers such as sweet peas and clematis, to name just a couple, will appreciate it to clamber up. The wooden framework gives height in the garden and, depending on the shade of wood-preservative used, provides a splash of colour all year. The projects on pp20 and 26 also require obelisks and you can hone your skills here before moving on to them.

Difficulty Rating 🔨

Design Tip

The best way to buy the timber for these projects is to bulk purchase roofing batten. One pack of roofing batten 84 x 1 x ³⁄4in (2134 x 25 x 19mm) should be sufficient for you to make several of the designs shown.

Tools

Pencil, expanding rule, carpenter's square, Jetcut panel saw, bradawl, drill, drill bits and countersink, screwdriver.

Sundries

Zinc-plated supascrews (1¼in/32mm No. 7), packaging tape, glue, wood-care product.

OBLONG TRELLIS

Dimensions

84 x 14in (2134 x 356mm)

Cutting List

Verticals	3	84 x 1 x ³⁄4in (2134 x 25 x 19mm)
Horizontals	10	14 x 1 x ³⁄4in (356 x 25 x 19mm)

Construction

1 Select three 84in (2134mm) long battens and with a length of packaging tape fix them together. Using the ruler, pencil across all the battens to give the positions of the ten horizontal battens. Use the Jetcut saw or a carpenter's square to mark these 90 degree lines.

2 Using a pencil, mark out along a length of batten the ten 14in (356mm) horizontal struts. Hold the batten firmly on the bench or table and using the Jetcut saw, cut the battens to length.

3 Now take all ten horizontal battens and tape them together. Using the saw or a carpenter's set square make pencil marks right across them to show the positions of the screws.

4 Using a hand drill or bradawl, bore holes in the horizontal battens. Get all the boring done before you start fixing things.

5 The simplest way to fix the trellis together is to lay the three vertical battens on the floor and, using the lines already pencilled-in on these, place the ten horizontal battens in position. Start by fixing the horizontal battens that go at each end of the vertical battens. This will keep everything in place while all the rest of the horizontal battens are being attached. It is worth putting a spot of water-resistant glue between each joint before you drive the screws through the pre-prepared holes into the battens beneath.

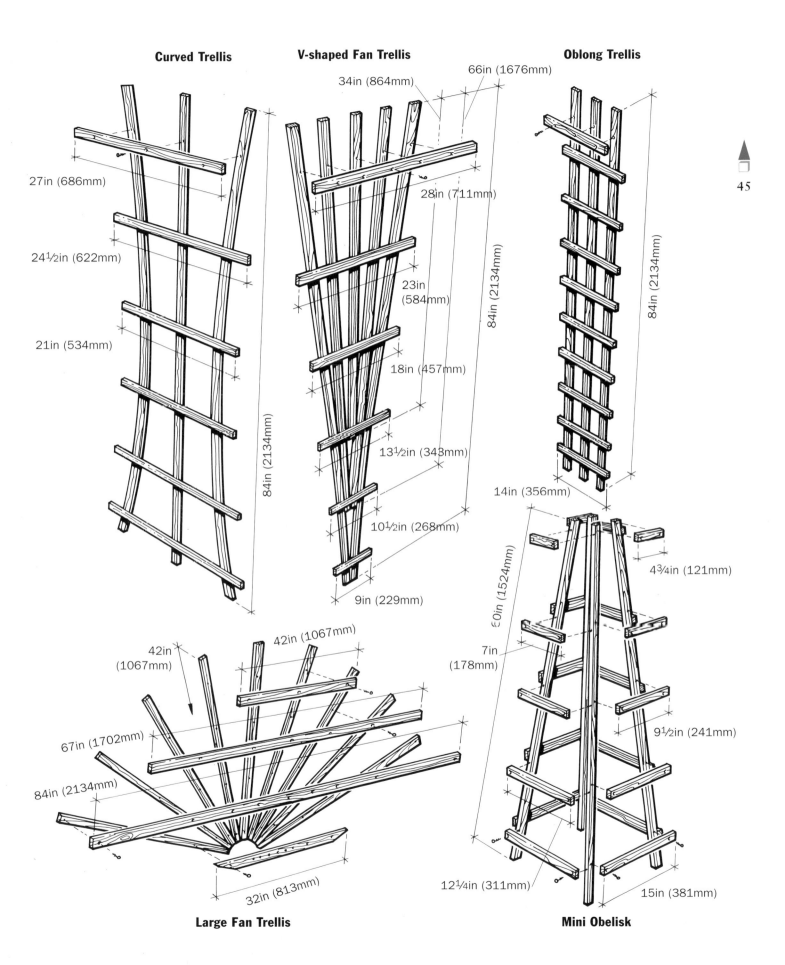

Curved Trellis

27in (686mm)

24½in (622mm)

21in (534mm)

84in (2134mm)

V-shaped Fan Trellis

34in (864mm)

66in (1676mm)

28in (711mm)

23in (584mm)

18in (457mm)

13½in (343mm)

10½in (268mm)

9in (229mm)

84in (2134mm)

Oblong Trellis

84in (2134mm)

14in (356mm)

Large Fan Trellis

42in (1067mm)

42in (1067mm)

67in (1702mm)

84in (2134mm)

32in (813mm)

Mini Obelisk

4¾in (121mm)

60in (1524mm)

7in (178mm)

9½in (241mm)

12¼in (311mm)

15in (381mm)

V-SHAPED FAN TRELLIS

Dimensions

84 x 28in (2134 x 711mm)

Cutting List

Verticals	2	84 x 1 x ¾in (2134 x 25 x 19mm)
	2	66 x 1 x ¾in (1676 x 25 x 19mm)
	1	34 x 1 x ¾in (864 x 25 x 19mm)
Horizontals	1	28 x 1 x ¾in (711 x 25 x 19mm)
	1	23 x 1 x ¾in (584 x 25 x 19mm)
	1	18 x 1 x ¾in (457 x 25 x 19mm)
	1	13½ x 1 x ¾in (343 x 25 x 19mm)
	1	10½ x 1 x ¾in (268 x 25 x 19mm)
	1	9 x 1 x ¾in (229 x 25 x 19mm)

Construction

1 Start by selecting two 84in (2134mm) long battens. If possible choose two that are fairly free from knots, otherwise there is a good chance that when you start to bend them, they will crack. Tape them together and pencil in the positions of the six horizontal battens.

2 Now bore two holes about 4in (100mm) apart at the base of one of these long battens and then screw both long battens together at their bases. Do not forget the glue.

3 Prepare the 28in (711mm) top batten with all the holes bored and screws at hand.

4 For the next operation you will need an assistant and a length of spare batten. Take firm hold of both battens at the top end and spread them apart. This is far simpler than it sounds – don't overstretch the battens.

With your assistant at hand, slip the spare batten between the spread battens and then place the prepared top batten on the pre-marked pencil position guides and screw it in place. You may have to juggle the spread of the battens, and the spare batten holding them, until the screw holes on the horizontal batten line up with those on the vertical battens. Keep your assistant handy until you have done this.

5 Remove the spare batten and you will be happily surprised to find that things will stay put. Now screw the remaining five horizontal spars in place.

6 The three remaining vertical spars can now be fitted and glued and screwed into place.

CURVED TRELLIS

Dimensions

84 x 27in (2134 x 686mm)

Cutting List

Verticals	3	84 x 1 x ¾in (2134 x 25 x 19mm)
Horizontals	2	27 x 1 x ¾in (686 x 25 x 19mm)
	2	24½ x 1 x ¾in (622 x 25 x 19mm)
	2	21 x 1 x ¾in (534 x 25 x 19mm)

Construction

1 As with the other trellises, make a start by selecting two 84in (2134mm) battens that are fairly knot-free. Knots towards the ends are not a great problem, but in the middle of the battens they can be critical.

2 Take the two 27in (686mm) horizontal battens that go at either end of the trellis and bore the screw holes as indicated in the diagram on p45. Fix these to the long vertical battens: do not use glue at this point. You now have a long, rather floppy, rectangular trellis.

3 Prepare holes in the two 21in (534mm) horizontal battens and put them on one side. You now have to bend the trellis verticals to fit these in place.

Tie a piece of strong cord around the middle of the trellis, make a loop in the cord, insert a spare length of batten and wind it up like a tourniquet. Care is needed, and an extra pair of hands at this point is vital. Do not let go of the batten, otherwise you will get very sore fingers as it unwinds.

Keep winding until you have a nice concave curve, and the pre-prepared screw holes in the horizontal battens nicely line up with the curves in the verticals. (This may sound a little technical but it is not really hard to achieve.) Carefully place the trellis flat (still holding firmly on to the tourniquet winding batten) and, with the help of an assistant, place a spot of glue underneath the horizontal battens and screw them in place. While things are still in tension, fix the remaining horizontal battens – the 24½in (622mm) ones.

4 Finally very carefully unwind the tourniquet. Glue and screw the final vertical batten in place on the trellis.

LARGE FAN TRELLIS

Dimensions
84 x 42in (2134 x 1067mm)

Cutting List

Fan	9	42 x 1 x ¾in (1067 x 25 x 19mm)
Horizontals	1	42 x 1 x ¾in (1067 x 25 x 19mm)
	1	67 x 1 x ¾in (1702 x 25 x 19mm)
	1	84 x 1 x ¾in (2134 x 25 x 19mm)
	1	32 x 1 x ¾in (813 x 25 x 19mm)

Construction

1 The main skill with this trellis is spacing things out.

From the diagram, cut all the battens to length and position them on a flat surface.

First form the fan section. You can use a rule, but you will soon discover that the eye is the most accurate measuring tool in this case. Once you are happy with the arrangement of the fan of battens, put the horizontal battens in place and pencil in the positions for the screws.

2 Mark the angles on the bottom batten with a pencil. (It is the only one that requires angles.) Then carefully take the batten off the arrangement and use the Jetcut saw to do the shaping.

3 Now fix the pieces together. A spot of glue beneath each horizontal batten will ensure the trellis construction is rigid once complete. As you drive the screws into place be careful not to disturb the battens beneath.

MINI OBELISK

Dimensions

Height	60in (1524mm)
Width	15in (381mm)
Depth	15in (381mm)

Cutting List

Verticals	4	60 x 1 x ¾in (1524 x 25 x 19mm)
Horizontals	4	15 x 1 x ¾in (381 x 25 x 19mm)
	4	12¼ x 1 x ¾in (311 x 25 x 19mm)
	4	9½ x 1 x ¾in (241 x 25 x 19mm)
	4	7 x 1 x ¾in (178 x 25 x 19mm)
	4	4¾ x 1 x ¾in (121 x 25 x 19mm)

Construction

1 Tape together the 60in (1524mm) lengths of batten for the verticals and, either using a Jetcut saw handle or a carpenter's square, mark the positions for the horizontal battens across all four of the vertical battens.

Remember that you need to leave approximately 8in (203mm) at the bottom to provide sufficient leg length for the structure to be pushed down into soil: you don't want the first puff of wind to blow it over. The remaining battens can be spaced equidistantly up the tower, although the specified lengths of each batten (refer to the cutting list and diagram) will restrict your choice somewhat.

Break the tape, separating the legs into pairs.

2 Bore holes at the ends of each horizontal batten. A bradawl will do the job but, as the hole is close to the edge, there is a tendency for the screw to split the timber, so a drilled hole is to be preferred.

3 Take a pair of legs and position the bottom and top horizontal battens in place, forming a large A-shaped frame. Put a spot of glue beneath each batten and then drive the screws in.

4 Fix the rest of the battens in the same way.

5 You now have to form the second A-shaped frame. A very simple and accurate way of doing this is to lay the second pair of vertical battens on to the first A-shaped frame and repeat

the procedure described in steps 3 and 4. You now have two 'A' frames.

6 A second pair of hands is called for at this point, as both 'A' frames have to be held steady while the remaining battens are screwed in place above or below the existing fixed 'A' frame battens, as shown in the diagram (p45). If the battens were placed in line with the original 'A' frame battens, there would be a real chance that the screws would run into each other and split the batten. If you find that there is a tendency for the timber to start splitting as the screws bite home, bore the holes a little bit deeper, or use a bradawl to enlarge them.

FINISHING

For all the trellis designs, to finish use a wood care product as described on p18.

WALL FIXING

To fix any of the trellis designs to the wall, first drill a pilot hole at top and bottom of the vertical battens. Position the trellis on the wall and mark through the pilot holes on to the wall beneath, then remove the trellis. Fit a masonry bit to your drill and bore holes in the wall where they are marked – remember to wear safety specs. Insert plastic rawlplugs into the drilled holes and then drive screws through the battens into

ARCHWAY

In the garden, arches can be used to form a focal point, or as a natural break between one area and another. Once a sturdy archway has been positioned and established, it can become the foundation for lengths of trellis to be attached at either side.

Entrances in gardens do not come in stock sizes, and I feel it is always good to do a made-to-measure job if possible. I have made this design to be adaptable, within reason, so you can add to its height or width to make it fit the opening you have in mind. You will need to measure carefully and increase or decrease all the timber lengths accordingly, but the construction techniques will be the same for an archway that is 2½ft (75cm) wide as they are for a 3ft (90cm) one.

I think gardeners are often put off by the thought of building an arch: there seems to be something rather daunting about it. Well, this is a design that holds no unforeseen woodworking terrors.

Difficulty Rating

Dimensions

Height	81in (2057mm)
Width	37½in (952mm)
Depth	30in (762mm)

Design Tip

Read through the instructions before cutting timber. To alter the dimensions of the arch, extend the length of the curved front and back pieces and the three battens at the top. The side sections remain the same as before.

Tools

Pencil, expanding rule, clamps, Jetcut panel saw, jigsaw or coping saw, drill, drill bits and countersink, bradawl, screwdriver, hammer.

Sundries

Zinc-plated supascrews (1½in/38mm No. 8), glue, packaging tape, sandpaper, wood-care product, four metal socket posts.

Cutting List

THE SIDES

Main uprights	4	81 x 2 x 2in (2058 x 50 x 50mm)
Top and bottom cross pieces	4	30 x 3 x ⅞in (762 x 76 x 22mm)
Batten – trellis verticals	12	70 x 1 x ¾in (1778 x 25 x 19mm)
Batten – trellis horizontals	10	30 x 1 x ¾in (762 x 25 x 19mm)

THE TOP

Curved front and back	2	35¾ x 4 x ⅞in (908 x 102 x 22mm)
Batten – trellis	10	30 x 1 x ¾in (762 x 25 x 20mm)
Batten – trellis	3	37½ x 1 x ¾in (953 x 25 x 20mm)

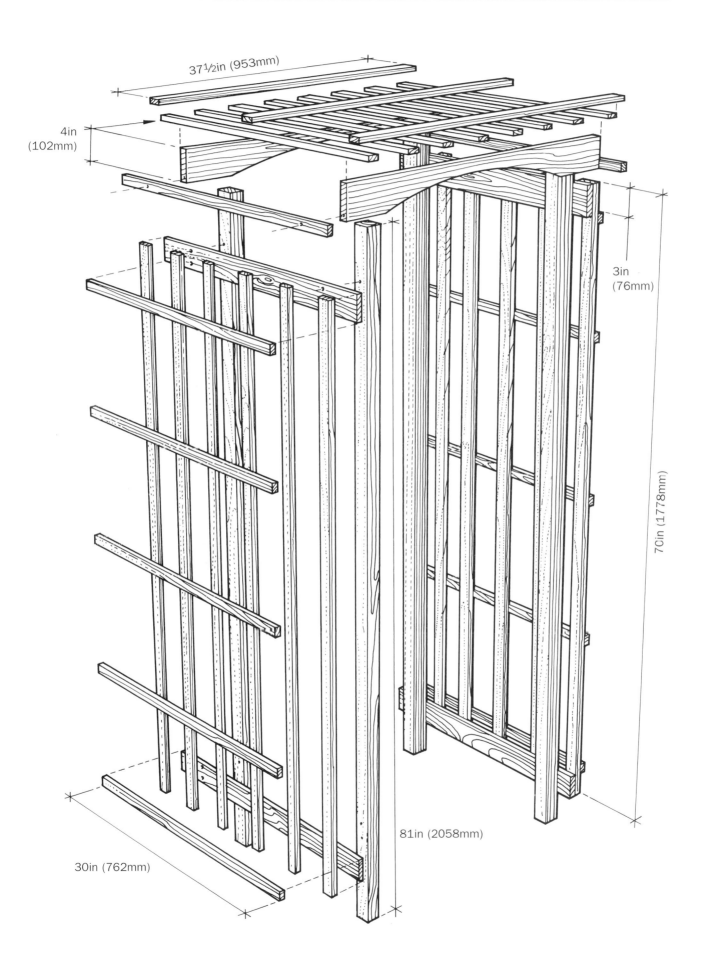

37½in (953mm)

4in
(102mm)

3in
(76mm)

70in (1778mm)

81in (2058mm)

30in (762mm)

Construction
THE SIDES

1 Fasten the four main uprights together with clamps or packaging tape and mark in pencil where the four main cross pieces are to go. Then fasten together the top and bottom cross pieces and mark in pencil where the uprights are to go.

2 Assemble the cross pieces with the uprights to make what are effectively two large wooden rectangles – the sides of the arch. Make the first rectangle by drilling and countersinking holes in all the cross pieces, then positioning two of the uprights with two of the cross pieces – one at the top, the other at the base – and screw and glue them in place.

3 Check for squareness. The simplest method is to use a batten to check the distance between the diagonal corners. A piece of string will do, providing you have an assistant at the other end. Once you are satisfied that the corners of the first rectangle are square, you can build the second one using the first as a handy guide.

4 Measure and cut 12 lengths for the trellis verticals. Bore two holes in either end of each piece, then glue and screw them on to the cross pieces, six battens on each large rectangle.

5 Now cut ten batten lengths for the trellis horizontals, gluing and screwing five per side on to the six vertical battens. The two sides of the arch are now complete.

THE TOP

1 To form the curved arch at the top you need a coping saw or a jigsaw. Once you have cut your timber to length, mark out the curve using a piece of batten (see p34, trough, step 2) or a template (see p16). Clamp the timber firmly to the bench and cut out the shape. Use sandpaper to remove the saw cuts.

2 Now cut ten battens of equal length for the trellis work over the top of the arch. Tape them together and pencil a line across them at either end to mark where the screw holes should be made. Bore all the holes in the battens.

3 Assemble the arch top on a flat surface with the help of an assistant at the initial fixing stage. Glue and screw the two battens that go on the sides of the curved pieces first and then those that go on either end, and then space and attach the remaining six at regular intervals.

4 To finish off the arch top, a further three battens are screwed on to the existing ones, at a 90 degree angle to them.

ASSEMBLY

1 The top is now fitted on to the uprights. Please do not be tempted to do this with the arch upright. Get an assistant to hold the two upright sections on their sides on the ground, and then position the top on to them. Bore holes through the uprights and screw the top into place. Ideally use two screws per side to make a good fixing.

2 Do not rush to lift the arch into the air, as arches are very vulnerable at the base until they are fixed in the ground. Select a waste piece of batten and screw it across the bottom of the arch opening. This will stabilize the sides until the arch is fitted into the ground, preferably using metal socket posts, which have a long spike on one end and a socket to accept timber on the other. They also have holes so that the timber can be screwed firmly into them.

3 Measure out where the arch legs will go and, wearing safety specs, drive the four sockets into the ground.

Now, with your assistant to help, lift the arch into the air and plant the four feet firmly into the sockets and screw in place. An arch sited in this way will not blow over in strong winds.

FINISHING

Use a wood-care product as described on p18. This is best done before siting the arch.

COLDFRAME

58

Coldframes are very useful for bringing on seedlings, not just providing shelter from cold rain and wind, but also giving a degree of protection from garden pests. For the lights, I recommend that you use acrylic 'glass', as this is resistant to the sun's rays and does not embrittle so quickly as other materials. Its other great advantage is that it is hard and does not scratch too easily, so a wipe and a wash with a clean cloth will not mark the surface.

I have used tongue and groove boarding, with a relieved edge, for the box. Some timber merchants call this decorative tongue and groove board but, in this case, the edge is not only decorative: it also allows water to drain away more easily. Tongue and groove boarding is also the simplest method of building wooden walls for this kind of project as the pieces slot together very readily.

Difficulty Rating 🔨 🔨

Dimensions

Height	15in (381mm)
Width	50in (1270mm)
Depth	24in (610mm)

Design Tip

This project has one of the few joints in the book: the lid frame consists of four pieces of timber that have halving joints cut on all ends. These allow all the pieces of wood to lie flush with each other and makes fixing the acrylic sheet, which is used as the light, very simple.

Tools

Pencil, expanding rule, carpenter's square, marking gauge, Stanley knife, Jetcut tenon saw, surform tool, bradawl, drill, drill bits and countersink, screwdriver.

Sundries

Zinc-plated supascrews (1½in/38mm No. 8), zinc-plated coach bolt, screw eyes, nylon cord, three self-recessing brass hinges, wood-care product.

Cutting List

BASE		
Front and Back T&G board with cut-back edge	5	48 x 4½ x ⅝in (1220 x 114 x 16mm)
Sides T&G board (as above)	6	22 x 4½ x ⅝in (559 x 114 x 16mm)
Corner posts – back	2	12½ x 2 x 2in (318 x 50 x 50mm)
Corner posts – front	2	8¼ x 2 x 2in (210 x 50 x 50mm)
Bottom battens	2	49 x 2 x 2in (1245 x 50 x 50mm)
Bottom battens	2	20½ x 2 x 2in (521 x 50 x 50mm)
LID		
Frame back and front	2	48 x 2 x 1in (1220 x 50 x 25mm)
Frame ends	2	24 x 2 x 1in (610 x 50 x 25mm)
Side strips	2	24 x 2 x 2in (610 x 50 x 50mm)
Handle	1	8 x 2 x 1in (203 x 50 x 25mm)
Sheet of acrylic		48 x 24in (1220 x 610mm)

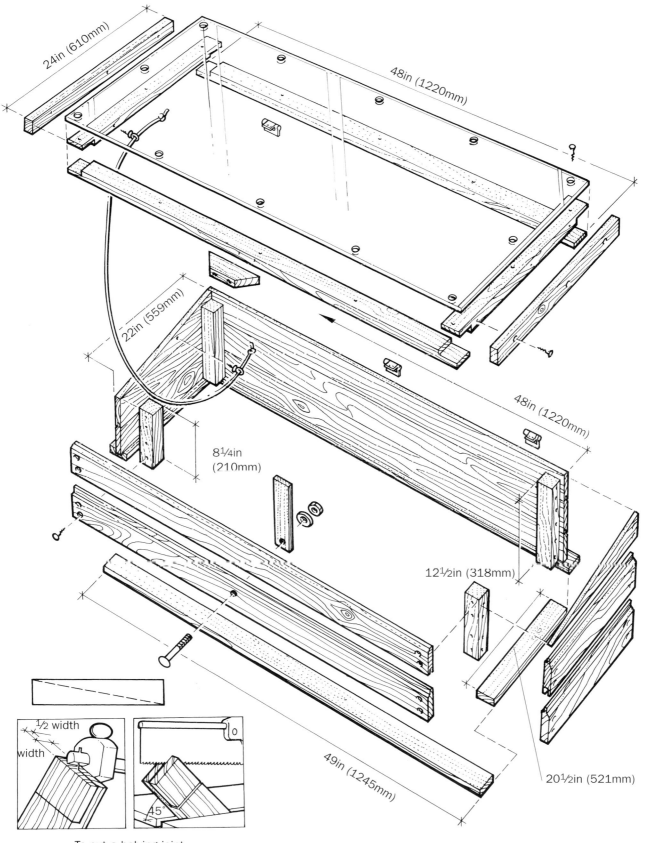

24in (610mm)

48in (1220mm)

22in (559mm)

8¼in (210mm)

48in (1220mm)

12½in (318mm)

49in (1245mm)

20½in (521mm)

½ width

width

45°

To cut a halving joint

Construction
BASE

1 Cut to length the two back and two front corner posts. Then the T&G boards: three for the back, two for the front and three for each of the sides.

2 Assemble the two front T&G boards. Before you fit them together, cut the groove off the lower edge of the bottom board. This board has a hole drilled centrally to take the lid stay.

3 Place the front corner posts on a flat surface. Drill and countersink holes in the ends of the front T&G boards. Now position them on the front corner posts. Overlap the boards on the posts by the thickness of the board so that when the side T&G boards are fitted they can lie flush with the front boards at the corners. Put a drop of glue on each board before attaching them.

4 Take the three back T&G boards and screw these on to the back corner posts, overlapping them in the same way as for the front boards and posts. Keep the bottom of the corner posts flush with the bottom T&G board.

5 The side T&G boards are now made up. Using a Jetcut saw, cut the top board along the diagonal, so that the sides will slope down from the back. Glue this shaped top board on to the board beneath. When the glue is cured (dry), bore holes at the ends of the T&G boards and then screw and glue them on to the corner posts: an assistant is useful at this point. Ideally keep the box on a large flat surface while you work and check for squareness as you go.

6 Now drill and screw the bottom battens around the base of the box, making sure that the screws go into the centre of the wood of the T&G boards to prevent them splitting. These battens will spend all of their life in contact with soil so at the finishing stage particular attention should be given to them. Roofing battens are ideal for this job as the wood-preservative keys well to their rough surface.

7 Shape the lid stay from a spare piece of batten, and use a small coach bolt to hold it in place on the front of the coldframe.

HALVING JOINTS FOR THE LID

To make the halving joints for the lid frame you need a sharp tenon saw, a marking gauge, a carpenter's square and a Stanley knife. Be logical about the whole operation.

1 Cut to length the four pieces of timber for the lid frame.

2 Start by marking the width of the timber on to all the eight ends with a pencil and square.

3 Now set up the marking gauge to measure half the thickness of the wood. The gauge has an adjustable wooden 'fence' that slides along a wooden rod with a spike in one end. By adjusting the wooden fence you can get the spike to score a line at this half thickness point. Score lines across the ends of the timber and down the sides.

4 Place the timber in the vice at 45 degrees and, keeping your eye on the gauge line as you go, saw down to the pencil mark that indicates the width of the timber. Now reverse the timber in the vice, re-positioning it at 45 degrees in the other plane – repeat the sawing operation.

5 Finally position the timber at 90 degrees in the vice and saw down to the gauge line. (The whole purpose of positioning the timber at 45 degrees for the first two cuts is to make saw paths that the saw blade can follow when the final cut at 90 degrees is made.)

6 Take the timber out of the vice and saw the cheek off, thus producing a joint that is half of the thickness of the wood.

7 Repeat for the other seven ends of the four pieces of wood.

LID

1 Fit the lid frame together without glue and check for squareness. Now use glue to stick the joints together. Small clamps can be clamped on the corners while the glue is drying.

2 Bore holes in the front spar to take the handle, which is glued and screwed into position. The handle itself is trimmed at 45 degrees on each end.

3 Position and screw the hinges to the underside edge of the lid frame and on to the outside edge of the back T&G boards.

4 The fittings for the acrylic sheet can now be put in place: the holes are bored to take the screws that will attach it, and you can position it on the frame, but final fixing should be left until the coldframe timber has been treated with wood-preservative. Acrylic sheeting takes holes very easily; if you have to cut it use a fine-toothed saw.

5 Prepare the two pieces of timber for the side strips and screw them on to the sides of the lid, making them overlap the coldframe sides.

6 Attach a length of cord to the inside of the lid and the frame using a hook eye and adjust it. This is to prevent the lid swinging backwards when it is opened and damaging the hinges.

FINISHING

Paint the coldframe with a wood-care product (see p18), paying special attention to the base, which will be in constant contact with damp soil, and then fix the acrylic sheet in place on the lid with screws.

POTTING BENCH

Working at the wrong height, be it at the kitchen sink or the workbench, will eventually cause backache, and in gardening will make what should be a pleasure a chore. Most practical jobs are accomplished more quickly and comfortably if the conditions are exactly right. This garden potting bench has both the height and space for working comfortably, and enough racks for you to store all the necessary equipment – pots, compost and rooting compound – that you might need while potting up.

The shelves at the back, above the bench top, are optional, but I find that you can never have too much storage space. It is also useful to have a back on the top of the bench: you can shovel up compost against it, and it will stop things falling off.

Difficulty Rating 🔫 🔫

Dimensions

Height 60½in (1537mm)
Width   36in (914mm)
Depth   24in (610mm)

Design Tip

Several coach bolts are used to hold this bench together. The holes for these must be very accurate so either get a friend to make sure that you are holding the drill at 90 degrees on both planes, or hire a drill in a drill stand, which will ensure they are straight. Hiring a drill stand from a tool hire shop is not very expensive and you will find it well worth the trouble.

Tools

Pencil, expanding rule, carpenter's square, clamp, Jetcut panel saw, surform tool, drill, drill bits, a countersink and a large flat bit, bradawl, screwdriver, adjustable spanner, round file, and, ideally, an electric drill in a stand (see Design Tip).

Sundries

Zinc-plated supascrews (1½in/38mm No. 8), packaging tape, six zinc-plated coach bolts and washers, glue, wood-care product.

Cutting List

BENCH BASE		
Legs	4	36 x 2 x 2in (914 x 50 x 50mm)
Bench top T&G board	4	36 x 5¾ x ¾in (914 x 146 x 18mm)
Bench surrounds	2	36 x 6 x 1in (914 x 152 x 25mm)
Bench surrounds	2	18 x 6 x 1 (457 x 152 x 25mm)
Leg braces	4	18 x 2½ x 1in (457 x 63 x 25mm)
Shelf slats	8	36 x 2 x 1in (914 x 50 x 25mm)
TOP SHELVES		
Shelves	2	36 x 6 x 1in (914 x 152 x 25mm)
Shelf backs	2	36 x 2 x 1in (914 x 50 x 25mm)
Shelf brackets	4	7 x 2 x 1in (178 x 50 x 25mm)
Shelf support legs	2	30 x 2 x 2in (762 x 50 x 50mm)

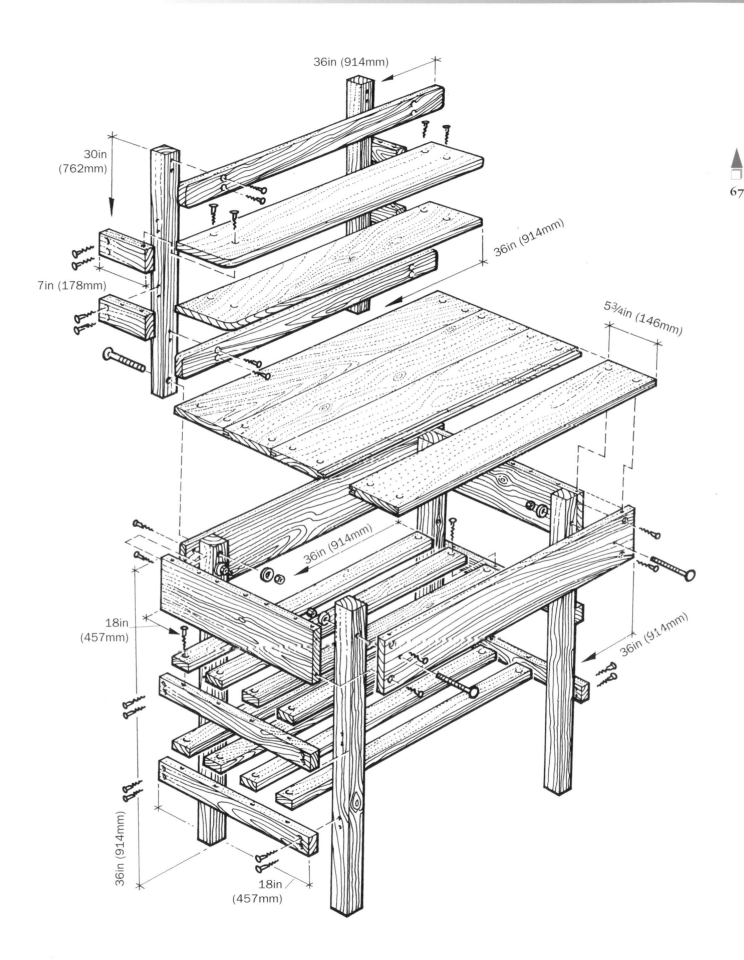

36in (914mm)

30in
(762mm)

36in (914mm)

7in (178mm)

5¾in (146mm)

36in (914mm)

36in (914mm)

18in
(457mm)

36in (914mm)

18in
(457mm)

Construction
BENCH BASE

1 Cut four legs to length, clamp or use packing tape to hold them together and then pencil across all four to indicate the positions of the two shelves and the holes for the bolts. Separate the legs and, using the carpenter's square, carry the pencil marks on around all four sides of each leg. It is so very much simpler to have a good pencil line to work to and it minimizes the chances of making any mistakes.

2 The bench top surrounds are made from four pieces of timber: front, back and two sides. The sides are set in from each end of the bench so, when the top is fitted, there are good hand holds to move it around.

Pencil in the positions for the screws and the bolt holes. The bolts are used to hold the bench legs to the bench top and the back shelf uprights to the back.

Bore the holes for the bolts using a drill stand (see Design Tip). You will need to bore these large holes accurately, which is more easily done before the sides and ends are screwed together.

3 Now glue and screw the front and back surrounds to the sides. Use some fairly lengthy

screws for this task (2in/50mm No. 8) as they have to hold in endgrain; gauge is also important. It is helpful to have a friend holding the pieces together while you work. When you fit the sides, doublecheck that there is room for the leg, and that the bolt holes line up.

4 The bench top is made from tongue and groove flooring board. The board nearest the front needs the tongue cut off, and when you have assembled the boards, you will see that it is best to remove the groove from the board at the back as this makes the job look much tidier.

Fit the back T&G board first, making sure it is flush with the back edge of the bench surround. Screw the boards down into the bench surrounds beneath them. The front board overlaps at the front edge, giving useful extra table space. Round off the front corners as sharp edges always cause grief.

5 Before the legs are bolted in place, it is best to attach the shelf support battens. Screw these on to the outside faces of the legs and line them up on the pencil marks made in step 1. It is very important you check that the legs and battens are square (i.e. all at

90 degrees to each other) and that, once the battens are fixed, the legs will just fit inside the bench top frame. At this stage of construction you can make adjustments but later on it is far more difficult.

6 Now make up the shelves from slats. At each end the slats are screwed on to a leg brace that runs at 90 degrees to the shelves.

7 Now fit the legs to the bench top. An extra pair of hands will be most welcome at this stage. If the bolt holes in the surrounds do not all line up exactly with the holes in the bench leg framework, use a large round file to open them out a little. Tap the bolts in place using a hammer and, before fixing the nut on the back, fit a large washer; this will prevent the nut head biting into the timber and will add considerably to the clamping action of the bolt on the leg and bench side. Once the legs are fitted, position the shelves. You will discover that they act as bracing for the legs, and will produce even more rigidity if you insert a couple of screws at each end.

TOP SHELVES

1 Hold both shelf support uprights together with a clamp or tape, and pencil in where the shelf brackets and the bolt holes will go.

Separate the uprights again and bore the coach bolt holes, then screw the shelf brackets on to the uprights.

2 Fit the table top back and upper shelf back, and screw the shelves in place on the shelf brackets. Then fit the shelf unit to the bench back with coach bolts.

FINISHING

It is vital that a wood-care product is used as most potting benches live outside (see p18).

TOOL CADDY

Gardening is supposed to be a relaxing hobby, but as you progress around the garden clipping, weeding and raking, it is all too easy to find you have left things behind leading to lots of unnecessary trips to the garden shed. This caddy is designed to take a variety of tools and two standard-size seed trays. You can also use it as a sack truck to wheel those monster bags of compost from the car boot into the garden.

What equipment you store on the caddy will really depend on what tools you have, and what you think it is appropriate to carry. I find that the large holes make excellent tool holders, and that everything from a trowel to clippers can be made to fit. I suggest that you sort out the tool shed (someone will be pleased), decide exactly what items you will find most useful to transport, and then, using a piece of card, experiment and see exactly what size holes will best accommodate which tools. Avoid hooks as I find that something always snags on these, and definitely no six-inch nails please.

Difficulty Rating

Dimensions

Height	39½in (1000mm)
Width	19½in (495mm)
Depth	22in (559mm)

Design Tip

It is important to get the holes for the wheel axle correct. An electric drill mounted in a stand makes drilling these holes at 90 degrees, in both planes, simpler and safer. Drills in stands are available from tool-hire shops at a very modest price. To be sure that everything will fit, buy the wheel and axle set before drilling any holes. It is simpler to apply wood preservative before you fix the wheels in place.

Tools

Pencil, expanding rule, protractor, carpenter's square, Jetcut panel saw, electric drill, drill stand, selection of different sized flat bits, drill bits and countersink, screwdriver, round file.

Hardware

Zinc-plated supascrews (1½in/ 38mm No. 8), glue, two wheels, a steel axle rod, two spring clips to hold the wheels on, terry clips, wood-care product.

Cutting List

TOP		
Main handle	2	36 x 2¾ x ⅞in (914 x 70 x 22mm)
Back stays	2	14 x 2¾ x ⅞in (356 x 70 x 22mm)
Top of main handle	1	14 x 2¾ x ⅞in (356 x 70 x 22mm)
Dowel rod handle	1	22 x 1in (559 x 25mm) diameter
Handle centre (with tool holes)	1	12½ x 2¾ x ⅞in (317 x 70 x 22mm)
Short tool arm	1	9 x 2¾ x ⅞in (229 x 70 x 22mm)
TRAY		
Sides	2	16 x 2¾ x ⅞in (406 x 70 x 22mm)
Front and back	2	15½ x 2¾ x ⅞in (394 x 70 x 22mm)
Slats for bottom	4	15½ x 2¾ x ⅞in (394 x 70 x 22mm)
LEGS AND ARMS		
Side arms	2	22 x 2¾ x ⅞in (559 x 70 x 22mm)
Front legs	2	15 x 2¾ x ⅞in (381 x 70 x 22mm)

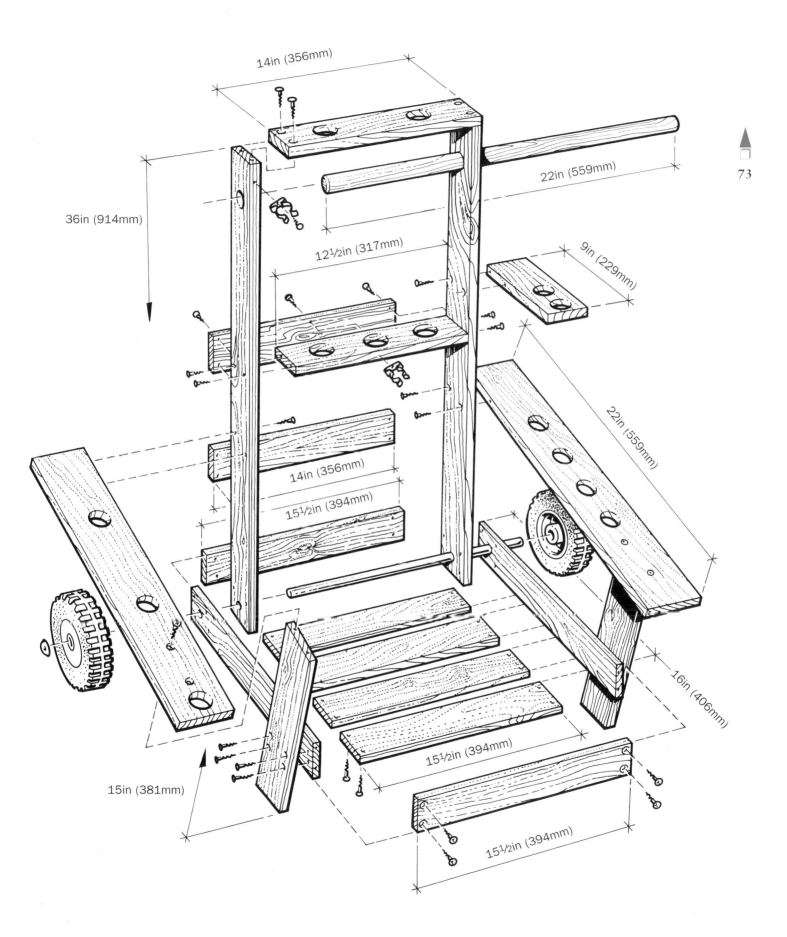

14in (356mm)

36in (914mm)

22in (559mm)

12½in (317mm)

9in (229mm)

22in (559mm)

14in (356mm)

15½in (394mm)

16in (406mm)

15in (381mm)

15½in (394mm)

15½in (394mm)

Construction

TOP

1 Cut to length the two verticals for the main handle. Tape them together and, from the drawing, mark in the axle hole position at the bottom, the back stays that brace the handle and the position of the large dowel rod handle at the top. Remove the tape and, using a pencil and carpenter's square, clearly draw in the lines where the various bits go.

2 Bore the holes to take the axle rod, preferably using a drill in a drill stand (see Design Tip). The simplest and least expensive wood boring bit is the flat bit, which was especially developed for electric drills and is ideal for large holes. However, boring tidy holes is best achieved by first drilling part way through the wood, releasing the drill bit from the timber, then turning the timber over. On the reverse side you will see that the tip of the flat bit has already emerged. Line up the drill tip in this hole and finish drilling. By boring from both sides you will achieve clean and neat holes. This is a useful skill as there are a lot of holes to drill on this job.

3 Having mastered the boring technique, make holes for the dowel handle.

4 Cut to length the main handle centre, the short tool arm and the main handle top. Now bore the tool holes in these. Cut the two back stays that fit on to the main handle section.

5 Before attempting to glue and fix any of the pieces above, fit the dowel rod into the pre-drilled holes at the top of the handle. If you find it is a bit of a squeeze wrap a piece of sandpaper around the part that is tight and sand it down a little.

6 Screw and glue the main handle top to the verticals. The centre piece is screwed into place from the outside of the main verticals. Glue the dowel rod in place at the same time as you glue and screw the back stays to the main handle (see diagram).

TRAY

1 Make the tray surrounds by cutting to length the four pieces of timber. The axle passes through the back part of the two

side members. The hole for it needs to be drilled – be careful to line it up with the existing holes in the bottom of the main handle. Now screw the tray surround together at the corners. Don't forget the glue.

2 Screw and glue into place the four slats that make up the tray base. Not only do these provide strength, but they also make a carrier platform for

peat sacks, buckets and a couple of standard-sized seed trays.

3 Thread the axle through one side of the tray, into the base of the handle and right through and out the other side of the tray. If it is reluctant to go through, use a round file to open up the holes and remove the obstruction. Once the base, handle and axle are threaded together, screw the two units together.

LEGS AND ARMS

As well as providing tool storage space, the arms and legs give rigidity to the handle and tray unit, which is very important if you are going to transport sacks of compost. Additional battens can be added to suit the tools you want to transport.

1 Make up the two front legs. Note the 7½ degree angle that has to be cut on their bottoms. Screw and glue them to the tray.

2 The arms are next. They have a variety of different-sized holes bored in them for the tool storage: bore these before fixing the arms to the caddy. Secure each arm to the top of a front leg with two screws and glue; two screws are also necessary to secure it to the main handle at the back.

3 Add any other tool battens, such as the short tool arm, which fits on to the left main vertical.

FINISHING

Use a wood-care product as described on p18. This is more easily done before fixing the wheels and axle in place.

BIRD TABLE

I am always looking for ways to encourage birds to come to my garden. Not only do they greatly enhance the immediate environment with their songs and their movement in flight, but they are such good gardeners, eating caterpillars and removing aphids from rose bushes and fruit trees. In mid-winter, when frosts strike, the birds need some help to get through the long winter days, and the provision of food and water can be critical for their survival.

I do not intend to advise you on what to feed birds but I can help you to build a good site, off the ground. Once the table is built and stocked with food it will take the birds a little time to adopt it as their feeding place. It is important to position the bird table away from trees, where a lurking moggy may launch an air strike. No matter how tall the post, unless you put a funnel-shaped barrier (made from a piece of wire netting) on it cats will be able to climb on to the bird table. It is unlikely that the cat will climb on to the table without the birds noticing but they may avoid the table for a while because of any lingering feline odour.

This is a good starter project as you can make it as simple or as complicated as you wish. A first time woodworker could make the post, legs and table and leave the roof off. The roof is an attractive addition and keeps food dry, but is just a little bit more complicated than the rest of the table. However, if you can get that far, why not spend a little more time and have a go at it? I am sure the birds will appreciate your effort on their behalf.

Difficulty Rating 🔫

Dimensions

Height	73in (1854mm)
Width	27in (686mm)
Depth	20½in (520mm)

Design Tip

Very early on you will need to consider how to fix the post upright. I have designed wooden feet for free-standing anywhere, but it is easy to buy a metal post socket that has a long spike in the end from a garden centre or DIY store. It is simpler to build the table top and roof structure before attaching the post.

Tools

Pencil, expanding rule, protractor, clamp, Jetcut panel saw, surform tool, drill, drill bits, screwdriver, hammer.

Sundries

Zinc-planted supascrews (1½in/38mm No. 8), glue, brass panel pins, wood-care product.

Cutting List

Post	1	54 x 2 x 2in (1372 x 50 x 50mm)
Feet	4	14½ x 5 x ¾in (368 x 127 x 19mm)
Table	1	15½ x 8½ x ¾in (394 x 216 x 19mm)
Table sides	2	14½ x 2 x ½in (368 x 50 x 13mm)
Table ends	4	3⅞ x 2 x ½in (98 x 50 x 13mm)
Table supports	2	19½ x 2 x ¾in (495 x 50 x 19mm)
Food bars	2	12 x 1½ x ¾in (305 x 37 x 19mm)
Roof supports	2	16 x 2 x 2in (406 x 50 x 50mm)
Roof ends	2	17 x 8 x ⅞in (432 x 203 x 22mm)
Shiplap roof boards (covering is 4in/102mm per board)	6	23 x 4½ x ½in (584 x 114 x 13mm)
Decorative roof hip	1	27 x 2 x ⅞in (686 x 50 x 22mm)

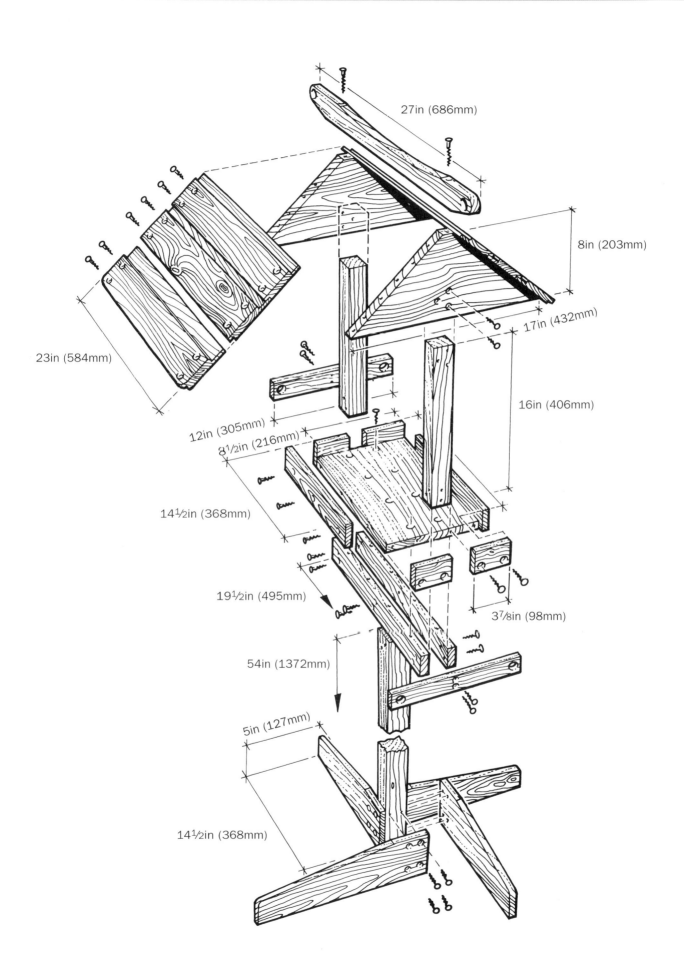

27in (686mm)

8in (203mm)

17in (432mm)

23in (584mm)

16in (406mm)

12in (305mm)

8¹⁄₂in (216mm)

14¹⁄₂in (368mm)

19¹⁄₂in (495mm)

3⁷⁄₈in (98mm)

54in (1372mm)

5in (127mm)

14¹⁄₂in (368mm)

Construction
POST AND FEET

1 You will see from the drawing and cutting list that the post and the roof supports are made from timber of the same dimensions. Select a length of wood that is straight-grained, and as free from large loose knots as possible. Cut the main upright post to length.

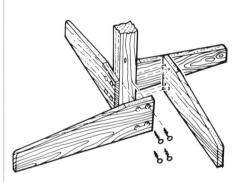

2 It is always a good idea to shape off the feet ends as it makes the finished table look so much more elegant. No joints are necessary to fix them to the post – simply glue and screw them on.

THE TABLE

1 The table is secured to the top of the post by the two support battens, which are screwed to the table top first. Check that the post will fit snugly between the battens then bore holes in the table top to take the screws. Now glue and screw the battens to the underside of the table, ensuring that they extend beyond the table top equally on both ends.

THE ROOF

1 The roof is held above the table by two upright lengths of timber. These are glued and screwed into the ends of the table support battens. Check that the uprights are at 90 degrees to the table top.

2 Make a cardboard template (see p16) of the triangle ends of the roof.

3 Using the card template, mark out two triangles on the timber and also mark in a centre line on the timber, and the positions of the holes you need to bore for the screws to secure the roof to the uprights. Clamp the timber to the bench then cut out the triangles using a Jetcut saw. Once both roof ends are cut out, use a surform tool to remove any saw marks.

4 Studying the diagram very carefully, mark out the correct positions for the screws that hold the shiplap boards to the triangular roof ends. It is simplest to put all the shiplap boards together and mark them all out together, using a rule and a long straight edge.

5 Now drill the shiplap to take the screws. The screws nearest the bottom edges of the shiplap need to be driven in very carefully, otherwise they may split the lower edges of the roof

triangles, which are quite a narrow angle. It is worthwhile boring small pilot holes in the triangles to accommodate these bottom screws.

Holding the ends in place and fixing the shiplap really requires the help of another pair of hands. Once the first few boards are in place it becomes fairly easy, but getting started is a bit more difficult.

6 The roof is finished off with a batten at the apex, attached with glue and screws. You can make this as simple or as complicated as you wish.

I used a jigsaw and a surform tool to cut out and shape up the batten for the top of my bird table, and then I bored a couple of big holes at the ends – just for a final effect.

ASSEMBLY

1 To prevent gusts of wind blowing the bird seed off the table, glue and screw small strips of timber along its sides. Don't make all the strips full length, but leave a gap so that old food and grain can be swept off and the table top washed clean.

2 To fit the table to the roof it is a good idea to have an assistant. The two upright roof supports from the table should fit flush on the inside of the two triangular roof ends. Position the uprights and ends and, with your assistant holding things together, drive a screw through an end piece and into an upright. To begin with fix only one screw at each end; check that all is well and fits neatly before you drive in all the other screws.

3 Now fit the post to the top of the table and the table support battens beneath, and secure with screws and a drop of glue.

4 I often find that scraps of food need to be tied on to the table. Make food 'hooks' using a couple of battens with large holes bored in the ends. Screw these to the roof supports where they meet the table support battens.

FINISHING

The table will need to be treated with a wood-care product (see p18). It is a good idea to get this done before winter as although many wood-care products produce little odour, birds have a very refined sense of smell. Once the table has been out for a few weeks and weathered in, they will adopt it as their feeding place.

TOOL STORE

No matter how tidy I try to keep the garden shed and return the tools to the rack after use, a few extra seed trays and terracotta pots, a length of hosepipe and a spare sack of potting compost soon invade the space, tools become dislodged from their allotted spaces and it is not long before I can't find anything.

In an attempt to rectify the situation I have designed a purpose-built tool store where there is a place for everything and everything is in its place. Forks, trowels, clippers and spades are now in regimental order.

The material used for constructing the store is basically tongue and groove floor boarding, which is easily obtainable and not too expensive.

Difficulty Rating 🔨 🔨 🔨 🔨

Cutting List

WALLS

Sides T&G board	6	50 x 5 x ¾in (1270 x 127 x 19mm)
Back T&G board	5	50 x 5 x ¾in (1270 x 127 x 19mm)

BATTENS FOR FRAMING

Back vertical edges	2	49¾ x 2 x 1in (1264 x 50 x 25mm)
Front vertical edges	2	47¾ x 2 x 1in (1213 x 50 x 25mm)
Sides – top and bottom edges	4	13 x 2 x 1in (330 x 50 x 25mm)
Back – top and bottom edge	2	26¾ x 2 x 1in (679 x 50 x 25mm)
Front – top and bottom edge	2	27 x 2 x 1in (686 x 50 x 25mm)

BASE

Batten for supporting floor	2	25 x 2 x 1in (635 x 50 x 25mm)
Feet	2	19 x 2 x 1in (483 x 50 x 25mm)
Floor T&G boards	6	14 x 4½ x ⅞in (356 x 114 x 22mm)
Tool support batten	1	24¾ x 2 x 1in (629 x 50 x 25mm)
Handles	2	15¾ x 2 x 1in (400 x 50 x 25mm)

DOOR

Door T&G boards	5	44¼ x 5¼ x ⅞in (1124 x 133 x 22mm)
Sill	1	25 x 2 x 1in (635 x 50 x 25mm)
Bracing battens		
Bracing battens – horizontal	3	24½ x 2 x 1in (622 x 50 x 25mm)
Bracing battens – angle	2	26¾ x 2 x 1in (679 x 50 x 25mm)

ROOF

Roof T&G boards	6	20 x 5½ x ⅞in (508 x 140x 22mm)
Fixing battens	2	30½ x 1 x ¾in (775 x 25 x 19mm)

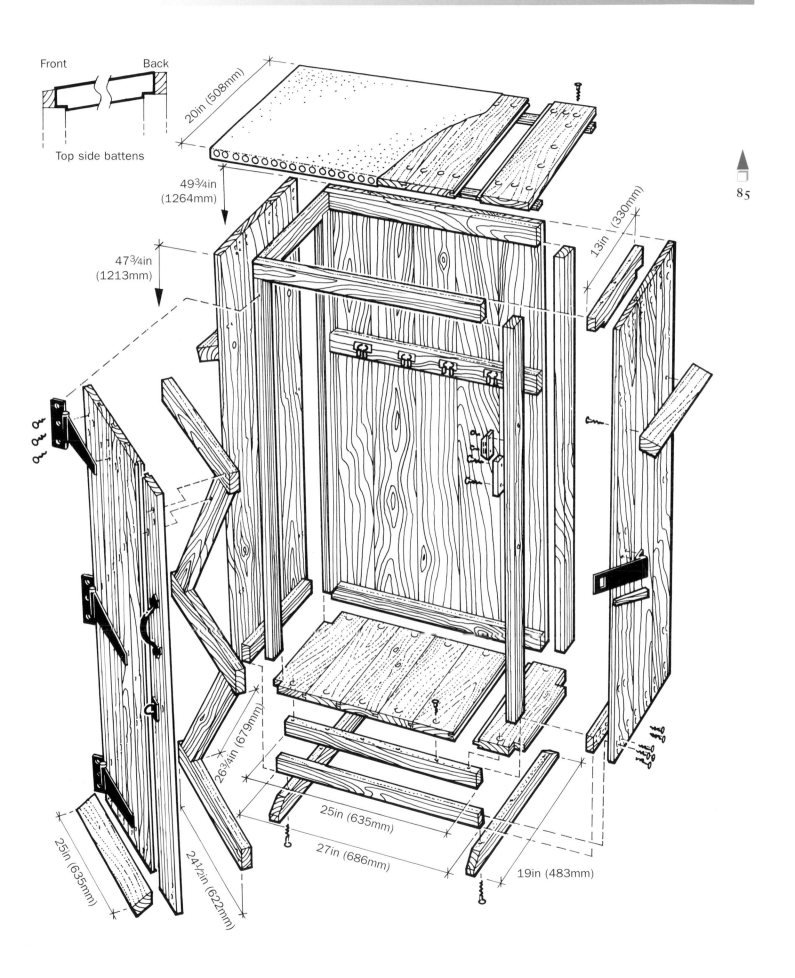

Front   Back

Top side battens

20in (508mm)

49¾in
(1264mm)

47¾in
(1213mm)

13in (330mm)

26¾in (679mm)

25in (635mm)

27in (686mm)

19in (483mm)

25in (635mm)

24½in (622mm)

Dimensions

Height   53in (1346mm)
Width   31in (787mm)
Depth   20in (508mm)

Design Tip

Do not be deterred by the rating of this project or its size. If you have worked through some of the other projects and honed your woodworking skills, then you can set about this task with confidence. This is a two-weekend job – at the very least.

Tools

Pencil, expanding rule, protractor, Jetcut fine-toothed saw, panel saw, plane, bradawl, drill, drill bits and countersink, screwdriver, hammer.

Sundries

Zinc-plated supascrews (1½in/ 38mm No. 8), glue, 3 T-strip hinges of 12in (304mm) long, a clasp, a handle, a magnetic catch, roofing felt, galvanized felt nails, terry clips, wood-care product.

Construction
WALLS

1 Make a start by cutting five T&G boards to form the back. Now screw battens across the top and bottom to hold the boards together. Care is necessary: you must hold the boards tightly together before fastening them to the battens. The screws are driven in from the outside and the battens are on the inside so it is helpful to make a pencilled line across the back to indicate where the screws are to go.

Once the back is made work begins on the sides.

2 Using three planks for each side, cut six lengths of T&G board to form the side walls. Make up these planks into two pairs of three. Pencil in the slope of the roof on the two pairs of T&G board and using a Jetcut panel saw, cut along this line. Screw battens at the base and top to hold the T&G board together. First screw a batten to the bottom (batten inside). Once again it is important to have marked a pencil line on the outside edge to guide where the screws go. Don't forget that there is a left- and right-hand side – otherwise you can end up with battens on the outside instead of the inside!

The top batten is slightly more complicated as it has to be trimmed at an angle at the back and front ends. The batten also requires a notch cut at the back,

which allows the corner batten (not fitted yet) to line up at the top. Cut back the front of the batten to the width of the batten that will run across what will be the doorway.

Study the diagram carefully to get this top side batten cut, angled and shaped correctly. When you are satisfied, glue and screw it in place.

3 Having made one back and two side walls you now need to attach them to each other. Cut two battens to length; these form the back corner fixing posts. Screw the battens to the T&G boards from outside in. Now screw the side walls to the same battens.

4 At the front, two battens are cut to fit the top and bottom of the doorway opening. The top of the top batten needs to be angled to fit the angle of the roof. I used some fairly long screws to fix the battens – 21in (75mm) No. 8 – driving them from the outside edges into the battens. Now two further battens are screwed to the front sides, forming the doorway. Do not forget to glue between all joints. These battens effectively complete the 'box' structure.

5 At the front, thicken up the batten on the bottom edge by screwing an additional batten behind it. Do the same on the back bottom edge. These two additional battens form the 'joists' for the planked floor.

BASE

1 Cut the six lengths of T&G board to form the floor. The corners of both outer planks have to be notched to accommodate the battens that form the corner posts. The boards are then fitted. It is only necessary to screw them at front and back, not at the sides.

2 To keep the whole structure off the ground, make up a couple of feet from two lengths of batten, and screw them on to the underside.

DOOR

1 Make the door from five pieces of T&G board. Reduce one piece of board in width to allow the door to fit in the opening. In this type of operation, the opening is measured and the door made to fit.

2 Simple doors like this one are held together by battens on the back. Horizontal battens are used and between them bracing battens, to take the strain as the door is opened and closed, are fixed at an angle. From the top side of the bottom horizontal batten, angle the lower bracing batten at approximately 45 degrees to the underside of the batten above. Cut 45 degree angles in both ends of the batten.

Repeat the angle on the next batten up. Glue and screw battens into place, fixing the horizontals first and then the angled ones.

3 To shed the rain running down the door away from the base cut a batten to the width of the door to make a sill. Hold it in a vice and plane an angle of 45 degrees on the edge. Then attach it to the bottom of the door by screws from the inside.

4 The door is hinged to the side with three large T-strip hinges. Ideally lie the whole structure on its back, position the door in the opening and screw the T-strip hinges in place.

5 Stand the unit upright, fix a handle and a locking padlock-clasp to the front. Inside fit a small batten to act as a doorstop.

It is also useful to fit a magnetic catch to keep the door closed when it is unlocked.

ROOF

1 Cut to length six pieces of T&G board for the roof. On the underside position two battens – back and front – and screw the T&G planks on to them.

2 Before fitting the roofing felt, screw the roof into the battens on the top of the tool store as shown in the diagram.

3 The roofing felt is best cut oversize to start with. You will find a Stanley knife ideal for cutting the felt and working on the corner folds. At the front edge fix a double fold of felt, and tack it down with galvanized felt nails. Stretch the felt to the back and repeat the folding and tacking operation. Then tack down the sides.

Make a neat corner fold with the felt.

FINISHING

1 Screw battens to the inside of the tool store and mount terry clips on them to hold the tools.

2 This is a fairly heavy piece of furniture so to make it more easily transportable construct some handles. These are made from two battens the length of the sides. Plane 45 degree angles on to them in a vice and then screw them to the outside of the box. These handles are angled in this way so that rain is shed off, and does not collect.

3 Paint with a wood-care product as described on p18.

BOX BENCH

Gardens are not just for working in – they are places to be quiet, to think, and to enjoy the beauty of your surroundings. I have more than one seat in my garden, and I like to move around them and spend time simply taking in the seasonal changes in different parts of the garden. My favourite hour for this is in the evening, just before the sun sets and when all the business of the day is over. I am sure that this little bench, made from Nordic red pine, will fit into any garden and prove a very welcome addition.

The 'box bench' concept must originally have been designed by a gardener, who wanted not just a quiet place to sit but also somewhere to store plant pots, a watering can and perhaps even a hosepipe. This design has the advantage that it can be 'stretched', so if you want a large box bench in which to store lots of useful items it can be extended by up to 12in (304mm).

Difficulty Rating 🔫 🔫 🔫

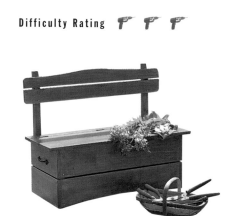

Dimensions
Height 36in (914mm)
Width 42½in (1080mm)
Depth 19in (483mm)

Design tip
For this project, it is particularly important that you study the drawing and cutting list carefully before you start, identifying each part, otherwise you will waste timber. If you take the cutting list to the timber merchant, this will make everything much simpler for you both!

Tools
Pencil, expanding rule, carpenter's square, clamp, coping saw (optional), Jetcut panel saw, jigsaw, surform tool or plane, drill, drill bits and countersink, bradawl, screwdriver.

Sundries
Zinc-plated supascrews (1½in/38mm No. 8), pair of handles, three brass-plated self-recessing hinges, sandpaper, glue, wood-care product.

Cutting List

Front and back boards	4	36 x 7½ x ⅞in (914 x 190 x 22mm)
Side boards	4	18 x 7½ x ⅞in (457 x 190 x 22mm)
Seat T&G board (5½in/140mm before T&G is cut off)	7	14½ x 5 x ¾in (368 x 127 x 19mm)
Front and back battens	2	32 x 1 x ⅞in (813 x 25 x 22mm)
Side battens	2	14 x 1 x ⅞in (356 x 25 x 22mm)
Front corner posts	2	18 x 2 x 2in (457 x 50 x 50mm)
Back corner posts	2	36 x 2 x 2in (914 x 50 x 50mm)
Seat boards	2	42½ x 7 x ⅞in (1079 x 178 x 22mm)
Seat board battens	2	10¼ x 3 x ⅞in (260 x 76 x 22mm)
Hinge board	1	42½ x 3 x ⅞in 1079 x 76 x 22mm)
Seat back rests	2	42½ x 4 x ⅞in (1079 x 102 x 22mm)

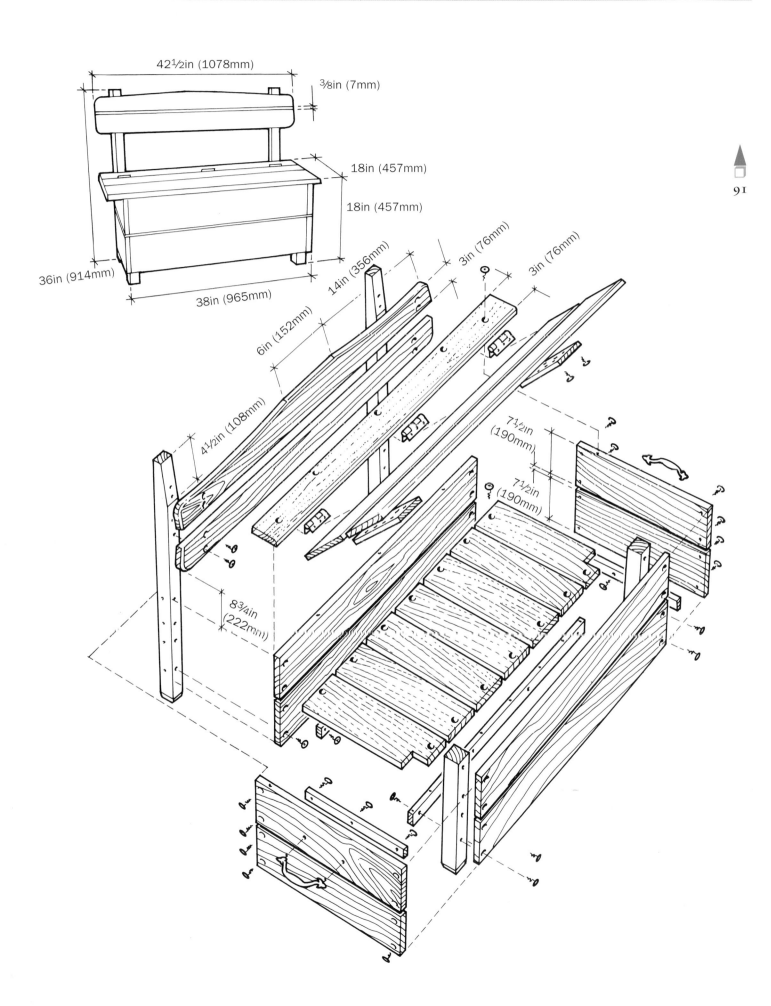

42½in (1078mm)

⅜in (7mm)

18in (457mm)

18in (457mm)

36in (914mm)

38in (965mm)

14in (356mm)

3in (76mm)

3in (76mm)

6in (152mm)

7½in (190mm)

7½in (190mm)

4½in (108mm)

8¾in (222mm)

Construction

BOX

1 Cut to length the two front and two back corner posts. Cut a chamfer on the bottom of each post by planing off the four edges at 45 degrees (see Design Tip p96 for further details). This limits damage when the bench is dragged across the ground.

2 Place the two front corner posts on your workbench, and then position the two front boards on the legs. Pencil in on the ends of each board where the screw holes are to be bored – two screws on the end of each board will be sufficient. Remove the boards from the posts and bore and countersink the holes for the screws.

3 Now carefully re-position the boards on the posts. Align the top board flush with the top of the first post, checking that board and post are at 90 degrees to each other. Place a drop of glue

between the two pieces and drive screws through the board into the post. The glue is slippery and there is a tendency for both pieces to move slightly, so check for squareness before finally screwing them together.

Repeat the operation at the other end of the board to attach the second post.

4 To avoid having to measure the gap between the boards, make a length of batten from an offcut to the correct width (⅜in/ 7mm). If you use this 'spacer batten', it will save you a lot of time.

5 Position the second board on the front posts and place a drop of glue between them. Slot the spacer batten between the two boards, check for squareness and then drive in all the screws to hold the second board in place. The front of the bench is now complete.

6 The two back corner posts need to be shaped at the top before the back boards can be attached. Referring to the diagram, pencil in the area to be removed, fix the post firmly to the workbench and saw off the angled section. Use a plane to remove the saw marks.

7 As with the front posts, lie the back posts flat on the work-bench, check the position of the

top board from the diagram, and glue and screw the two back boards on to the posts, checking for squareness as you work.

8 With the front and back of the 'box' completed, you will now need an assistant to hold the various pieces while you work on the side boards. Before you begin, bore and countersink all the screw holes in the four side boards.

9 With your assistant holding the back of the box steady on the workbench, glue and screw into place the two side boards for one end of the box.

This is quite easy, but do check that the boards line up with the back boards, and use the spacer batten to achieve the correct gap between them.

Now repeat the operation at the other end.

10 With the help of your assistant, lift the back up from the workbench and align the front of the box with the side boards. Glue and screw the front to the side boards, taking your time and checking for squareness as you work.

It is helpful if the box is positioned on a flat surface before you make this final assembly. You may have room on your workbench, but if not place it on the floor, which will help you align the side boards accurately with the front.

BACK RESTS

1 While the glue is drying, you can take the opportunity to shape up the back rests. I use a cardboard template, drawn up by looking at the diagram, to transfer the 'shaping' on to the wood for the top board (see p16). Cutting out the shape is not difficult, although if you use a coping saw you may work your way through a few spare blades before you get the hang of it.

2 Clamp the timber firmly, and start sawing along the pencil line. If you have an electric jigsaw, the job will be done in minutes, but again you must make sure you clamp the timber very firmly before you begin. Once the cutting is complete, use a surform tool and sandpaper to remove the saw cuts. Drill and countersink the holes for attaching the back rests to the back corner posts.

BOX BASE

1 In order for the base to be fitted into the box, a batten must be glued and screwed around the bottom inside edge. Turn the box upside down and follow the cutting list to prepare four battens to fix in place. Bore all the necessary screw holes in the battens and then, using glue behind the battens, screw them around the inside edge of the box. Keep the box upside down to work on the base.

2 I always look for simple solutions to woodworking projects. The slats which form the base of the box are actually cut from long lengths of tongue and groove spruce flooring boards. Being somewhat fussy, I cut off all the tongues and grooves (using a Jetcut saw and smoothing off with a surform tool or plane) to make the base look tidy. The boards are fitted as slats, with gaps between them, to allow water to escape and air to circulate, thus preventing the timber from rotting. One screw in the end of each board is sufficient to hold it in place on the batten. Before you can fix the boards at either end, you will need to cut out a small square section with a Jetcut saw to allow for the front corner posts.

SEAT

1 The seat is made up from two lengths of board, held together on the underside by two short lengths of timber. These two battens are screwed to the underside of the seat boards and provide a firm anchorage for them. The seat is hinged to a batten at the back of the bench, which in turn is screwed to the box framework.

Study the diagram, then position the seat boards 'face' downwards on the workbench and screw the battens on to the back of them, 4in (102mm) in from the ends.

2 The seat must now be hinged to the board that will eventually be screwed to the box. Using self-recessing hinges means that you don't have to cut recesses for the hinge flaps – simply screw them to the back of the seat, and then in turn to the hinge board. When this has been done, secure the hinge board to the box with screws.

FINISHING

1 Glue and screw the back rests in place. I think it looks good to leave the tops of the back corner posts showing above the top back rest.

2 As you will have discovered, this is quite a 'chunky' bench so it is useful to fit carrying handles. I used some very attractive wrought iron ones that look in keeping with this country box bench.

3 The woodworking is now complete and it only remains to apply a wood-care product to prevent it from deteriorating (see p18).

BOX CHAIR AND TABLE

The little chair in this project follows the same construction principles as the box bench, however, it is not exactly half the width of the bench, as this would spoil the proportion. It is comfortable to sit on and will fit into a small corner of any garden, and the storage space is very useful. You could make the bench and a chair, and perhaps store the terracotta pots in one and keep the hosepipe and watering can in the other.

The small table is designed to match the box bench and box chair. It is quite adequate for a tray of tea, and the cakes can be put on the shelf beneath. I feel this table, which is simple in its structure, is a really useful addition to the set of garden furniture.

I have kept the construction as simple as possible. There are no mortice and tenons to be cut, as the legs are simply held in place by screws and glue. The design of the table means that this is a very strong 'jointing' method, and is similar in technique to that used for making the box bench and chair.

The design is adaptable, and if you want a longer table all you have to do is extend the top planks, lower shelf planks and stretcher rails, leaving the ends the same. Your table could easily be extended to 48in (1220mm) long.

GARDEN BENCH

It is traditional and useful, and no garden should be without it – a bench. Traditionally this was made by the village carpenter, with lots of woodworking joints, and dowel rods used as pegs to keep the joints together: not a screw in sight. Oak was the standard timber and would have been supplied from the local estate.

Although none of my materials are traditional, nor indeed the joints, I like to think that in this little two-seater I have captured the spirit of the woodworking evolution that has been going on in the last hundred or so years.

Difficulty Rating 🔨 🔨

Dimensions

Height	36½in (927mm)
Width	43in (1092mm)
Depth	22in (558mm)

Design tip

The bench is attractive in itself but, as a final touch, you can add a pre-shaped moulding to the front seat slat if you wish. I think it is very effective. The choice of moulding is yours.

Tools

Pencil, expanding rule, protractor, Stanley knife, clamps, Jetcut panel saw, jigsaw, surform tool, drill, drill bits and countersink, bradawl, screwdriver.

Sundries

Zinc-plated supascrews (1½in/38mm No. 8), glue, sandpaper, wood-care product.

Cutting List

BASE		
Legs	4	17½ x 2 x 2in (444 x 50 x 50mm)
Stretcher/Support Rails		
sides (lower)	2	20¼ x 2 x 1in (514 x 50 x 25mm)
sides (upper)	2	18¾ x 5¼ x ⅞in (476 x 133 x 22mm)
back	1	36 x 2 x 1in (914 x 50 x 25mm)
front	1	36 x 5¼ x ⅞in (914 x 133 x 22mm)
ARMS		
Rests	2	19½ x 3½ x ⅞in (495 x 89 x 22mm)
Rest supports	2	9¼ x 2 x 1in (235 x 50 x 25mm)
Triangular blocks	4	1¾ x 1¾ x ⅞in (44 x 44 x 22mm)
SEAT		
Slats	8	42 x 2 x 1in (1067 x 50 x 25mm)
Moulding for front slat	1	42 x 1in (1067 x 25mm)
BENCH BACK		
Supports	2	24 x 2 x 2in (610 x 50 x 50mm)
Upper slat	1	42 x 7 x ⅞in (1067 x 178 x 22mm)
Lower slat	1	42 x 2 x 1in (1067 x 50 x 25mm)

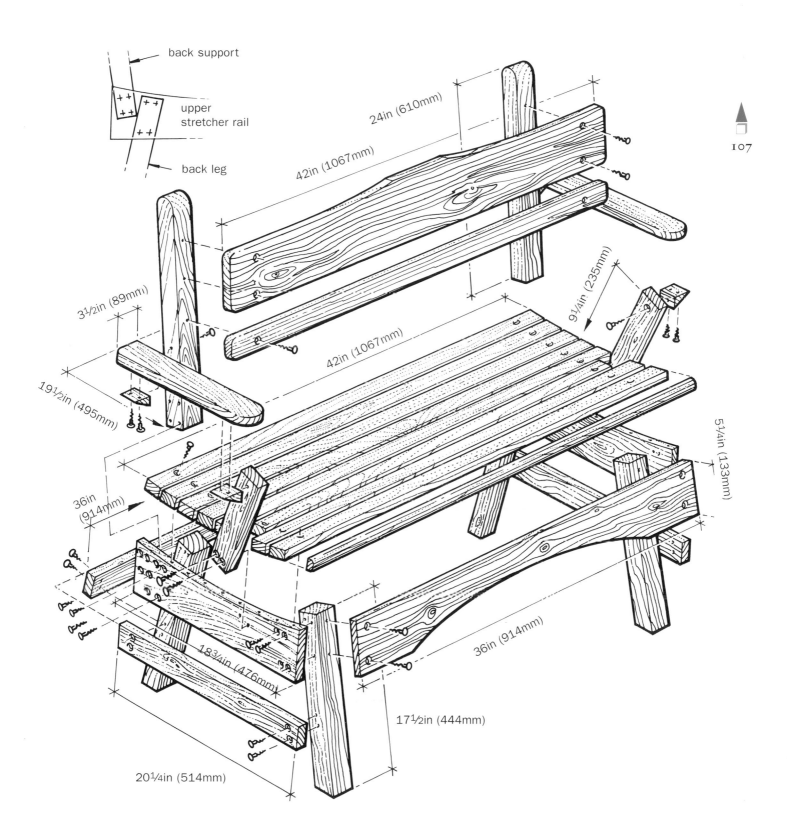

back support

upper
stretcher rail

back leg

24in (610mm)

42in (1067mm)

9¼in (235mm)

3½in (89mm)

42in (1067mm)

5¼in (133mm)

19½in (495mm)

36in
(914mm)

18¾in (476mm)

36in (914mm)

17½in (444mm)

20¼in (514mm)

Construction
BASE

1 Make a start by cutting four legs to length. From the diagram you can see the angles that are involved. It is best to get these cut on to the ends of the timber first. Once they are cut plane a little chamfer on to all four legs – it stops them splitting if the bench is dragged across the ground (see Design Tip p96).

2 On the legs, pencil in where the stretcher rails go.

3 From the drawing make a full size template (see p16) of the front and upper side stretcher rails. The two curved upper side rails (one at each end) hold legs, seat slats and back together.

   Once marked out use a jigsaw to cut the curved shapes and a Jetcut saw to cut the angles. Now drill and countersink all the holes.

4 To make up one end of the bench, line the legs up on the curved upper stretcher rails, and also the bench back supports. The bench back support posts need to be shaped off at the top before fitting. Aim to give them both a nice rounded end.

   Check the angles before and while screwing and gluing the legs and back support in position (the lower side stretcher rails are fitted later, see Arms and Seat step 3).

5 Make the second bench end by lining it up on the first so that both are identical. However remember that one is a left-hand side and the other a right-hand side so reverse the timbers.

ARMS AND SEAT

1 Now make the two arm rest supports, both gluing and screwing them on to the upper side stretcher rails. Note that these arm supports are glued to the outside face of the stretcher rails not to the back.

2 Cut out the front seat stretcher rail. For this you will need to use the jigsaw. After jigsawing be sure to remove all the rough sawn edges with a surform tool or plane, otherwise people's legs will get scratched.

   Also prepare the back stretcher rail, which is just a simple batten.

   With a helping pair of hands holding the two bench ends, glue and screw the front and back stretcher rails in place. At this point it is important to check that both ends (legs) are at 90 degrees to the ground.

3 Fit the lower side stretcher rails to the bench.

4 Cut to length the seat slats; a far more comfortable sit is assured if you plane off the upper edges with a surform tool or plane before fitting them. Space

the slats on the curved upper side stretcher rails and glue and screw them in place.

BACK

1 Make a cardboard template (see p16) of the shape of the bench back. Transfer this shape on to the timber by drawing around it with a pencil and, using the jigsaw, cut it out. Work around the edges with sandpaper, removing sharp and rough edges.

2 Next shape up the chair arms. Round off the ends with a jigsaw and then, using a surform tool, plane off the saw marks.

Pay particular attention to the edges making sure that they are nice and smooth.

3 Bore a hole through the side of the bench back supports and a hole into the back ends of the arms. Glue and screw the arm rest to the bench. Use a fairly long screw for this – say 3in (75mm) No. 8 gauge.

4 Cut the two small triangular blocks of wood to go beneath the arm rests at the back. This is easily done by marking a 45 degree line across the end of a piece of batten. Glue and screw

them in place. Now cut the two triangular blocks to go beneath the arm rest at the front. Gluing these blocks under the arms will greatly enhance their strength.

FINISHING

1 Add the pre-shaped moulding to the front seat slat if required. Simply glue the moulding in position and hold it in place with two or three pieces of tape while the glue dries.

2 Use a wood-care product as described on p18, paying particular attention to the base of the legs.

GARDEN BRIDGE

Now this is one of those projects that may look just a little ambitious if you are a beginner, and the question 'Will it work?' may just enter your mind. Have no doubts: this little bridge is very solid and capable of safely transporting any pedestrian over the deepest pond. However, bridges do not have to be placed across ponds. This one can be used as part of the walkway across a rockery. It can give height to a pathway or form a backdrop for a small garden.

You can fix hand rails on both sides of the walkway if you wish, but I like the single rail as it makes the bridge more open to view.

Difficulty Rating

Dimensions

Height	38in (965mm)
Width	72in (1829mm)
Depth	19in (483mm)

Design tip

The timber used can be either Nordic redwood or whitewood. Whitewood is probably easier to find in the width required to get a reasonable curve on the bridge side members. The main bridge members and treads need to be as knot-free as possible, especially in the centres of the treads as this will be where they get most stress when walked on. Knots at the ends are more acceptable. Buy rough sawn timber for the treads to give shoes a good grip.

Tools

Pencil, expanding rule, compass, Jetcut saw, jigsaw, surform tool (one with a curved sole would be helpful), drill, drill bits and countersink, battery-powered or Magnum screwdriver.

Sundries

Zinc-plated supascrews (1½in/38mm No. 8 and 1¾in/44mm No. 8), coach bolts, glue, cardboard for making templates, sandpaper, wood-preservative.

Cutting List

BRIDGE		
Side members	2	54 x 9 x 1in (1372 x 229 x 25mm)
Treads	23	18 x 1½ x 1in (457 x 38 x 25mm)
Keepers and feet	4	18 x 3 x 1in (457 x 76 x 25mm)
Upper keepers	2	16 x 1½ x 1in (406 x 38 x 25mm)
HAND RAIL		
Side posts	2	35 x 2 x 2in (889 x 50 x 50mm)
Centre post	1	33 x 2 x 2in (838 x 50 x 50mm)
Top rail	1	72 x 3 x 1in (1829 x 76 x 25mm)
Lower rail	1	60 x 3 x 1in (1524 x 76 x 25mm)

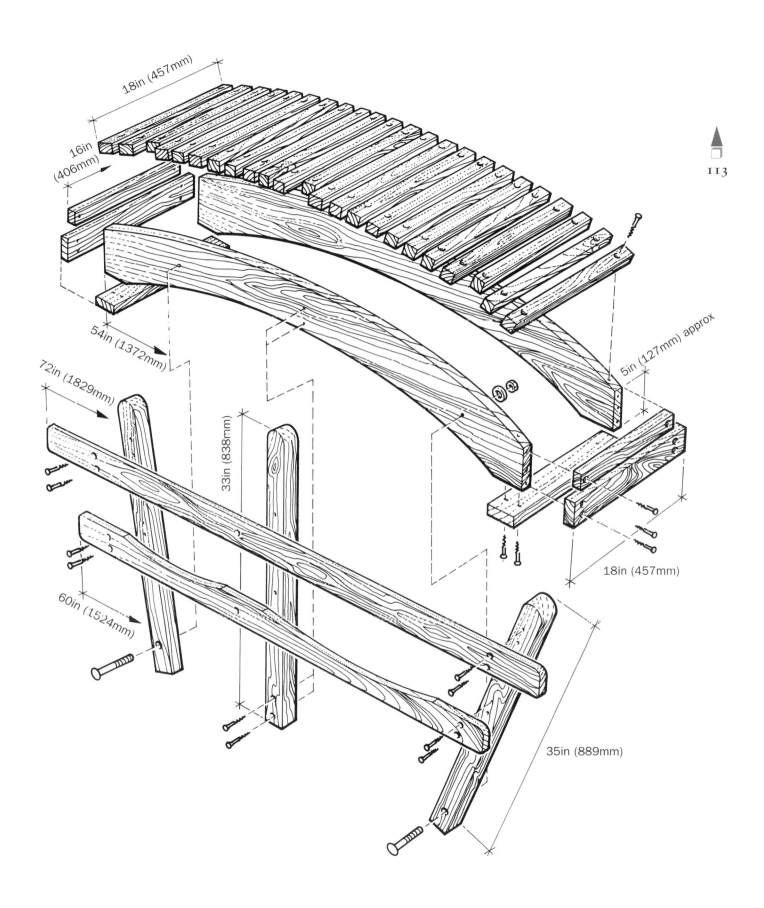

18in (457mm)

16in
(406mm)

54in (1372mm)

72in (1829mm)

33in (838mm)

60in (1524mm)

5in (127mm) approx

18in (457mm)

35in (889mm)

Construction
BRIDGE

1 Make a template of the curved shape (top and bottom curves) of the main members using a large piece of card (a section of cardboard box is ideal). The template only needs to be half the length of the members as you can use it to mark out from both ends. It is quite simple to use card in this way, and it prevents expensive mistakes with timber. You can choose how much of a curve to put on the bridge, but do not make the width of the centre too thin or you will severely weaken the finished structure.

2 Saw the main bridge timbers to length and, using your templates, pencil in the curves. Fix down the timber firmly and use a jigsaw to cut the shapes out.

As the jigsaw cuts along the pencilled lines, check periodically that you are not running the underside of the blade into your bench top.

Once the main bridge members are cut to shape use the surform tool with a curved sole to remove all the saw blade marks.

3 The keepers and feet now need to be screwed on to the ends of the main bridge members (see diagram). First bore screw holes in the pieces and then carefully position them, screwing and gluing them into place. Check that the sides are square with the ends, otherwise you will have a lop-sided bridge.

Once the two larger end battens have been attached, fix the others at both ends before starting on the foot treads.

4 Check the diagram: three of the foot treads are shorter than the others to accommodate the posts for the hand rail. Cut them to be flush with the main member on the hand rail side, about 1in (25mm) shorter.

Using a rule, establish the centre point of the bridge on both main members and indicate it with a pencil mark. Position and screw in place the centre tread, which is one of the shorter ones.

Now it is a matter of screwing all the other treads in place. Obviously it is quicker to drill and countersink all the holes in the treads before you start. Another useful time-saving device is a 'spacer batten' (see Box step 4 p92). This is placed against a tread that is already attached. The tread to be fixed is then butted up against the spacer batten, and glued and screwed into position. The spacer batten can then be removed and used to mark the next tread spacing. This prevents the irksome job of measuring the space between the treads each time: it is also quicker and more accurate. Towards the ends of the bridge remember the two shorter treads to fit the end hand rail posts.

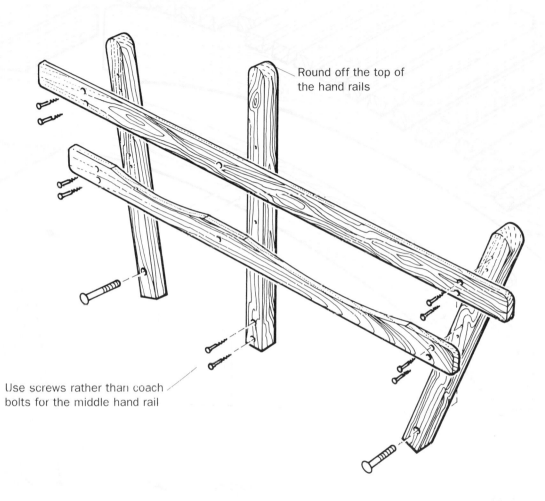

Round off the top of
the hand rails

Use screws rather than coach
bolts for the middle hand rail

HAND RAIL

1 The three posts now have to be worked in. It is important to round off the tops of the posts.

Mark out a half circle on the top of the posts using a compass and then use the jigsaw to rough out the shape. Use a surform tool to work over the tops of the posts, removing any saw cuts and smoothing off any sharp edges.

2 Glue and screw the centre post on to the centre of the bridge. I have avoided using coach bolts

here as it means boring a large hole in the centre and will weaken the bridge structure.

3 Coach bolt the other two posts in place. Don't forget to place washers behind the nut before assembly begins.

4 The hand rails come last. I have introduced a little shaping on the bottom rail, using a jigsaw to cut it out. Make a template as you did for the main bridge members (bridge, step 1) if

you want to make similar shaping. Take time to round off any sharp edges on the rail using a surform tool.

5 Glue and screw the hand rails in place. It is simpler to fix them to the centre post first. Then, using a spirit level, screw them into the two end posts.

FINISHING

Use a wood-care product as described on p18.

LOUNGER

This lounger is a real luxury, perfect to relax on in your garden after all the work is done. The design incorporates an adjustable head-rest so that you can prop yourself up and read if you wish. I have also put a gentle curve in the main bed section and this really does make it very comfortable. Because the project is large it may seem a little daunting, but if you have been working through this book you will already have had practice on all the different woodworking techniques: this project will simply stretch your already acquired skills.

The folding head-rest mechanism is similar to a small deckchair and requires some care, so study the diagram to avoid mistakes. The coach bolts must be zinc-plated, as standard mild steel bolts will rust and spoil the smooth working of the head rest. As the lounger is fairly heavy, you will find the addition of wheels a great benefit.

Difficulty Rating 🔫 🔫 🔫 🔫

Dimensions

Height   17in (432mm)
Length   70in (1778mm)
Width   20in (508mm)

Design tip

A careful study of the working diagram is essential. Pay particular attention to the head-rest section, which has several moving parts. At the timber merchant be prepared to be fussy and buy the best boards that they have for the side rails. Knots in the timber are acceptable, but make sure that they are 'living', that is, firmly attached to the surrounding timber.

Tools

Pencil, expanding rule, carpenter's square, clamps, Stanley knife, Jetcut tenon and panel saws, jigsaw, plane, electric drill, variety of drill bits, a large flat bit and countersink, screwdriver.

Sundries

Zinc-plated supascrews (1½in/38mm No. 8), four zinc-plated coach bolts (2½in/64mm long, ⅜in/7mm diameter), two rubber-tyred wheels, a steel axle rod, two spring clips to keep the wheels in place, cardboard for templates, sandpaper, glue, wood-care product.

Cutting List

BED		
Sides	2	68 x 5½ x ⅞in (1727 x 140 x 22mm)
Foot	1	18 x 5½ x ⅞in (457 x 140 x 22mm)
Legs	4	14 x 5½ x ⅞in (356 x 140 x 22mm)
Leg stretcher rails	2	68 x 2 x 1in (1727 x 50 x 25mm)
Cross stretcher rails	3	18 x 2 x 1in (457 x 50 x 25mm)
Blocks for wheel axle	2	5½ x 2 x 1in (140 x 50 x 25mm)
Slats	18	20 x 2 x 1in (508 x 50 x 25mm)
HEAD-REST		
Planks	4	20 x 6 x 1in (508 x 152 x 25mm)
Head	1	20 x 7 x 1in (508 x 178 x 25mm)
Head-rest support rails	2	26 x 2½ x 1in (660 x 62 x 25mm)
Prop rails	2	12 x 2¾ x 1in (305 x 70 x 25mm)
Dowel rods	1	16 x ¾in (406 x 20mm) diameter
Slotted rails for head adjustment	2	10¾ x 2 x 1in (273 x 50 x 25mm)

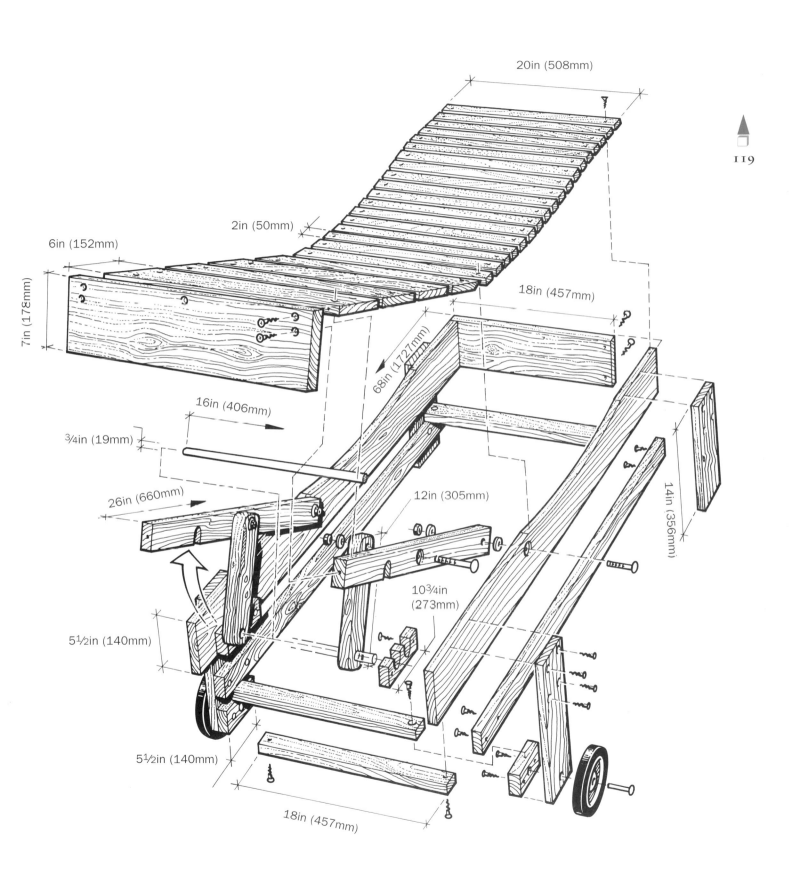

20in (508mm)

2in (50mm)

6in (152mm)

7in (178mm)

18in (457mm)

68in (1727mm)

16in (406mm)

¾in (19mm)

26in (660mm)

14in (356mm)

12in (305mm)

10¾in (273mm)

5½in (140mm)

5½in (140mm)

18in (457mm)

Construction
BED

1 Make a card template (see p16) of the curved section of the bed sides.

2 Clamp together the two bed sides. Using a carpenter's square, pencil in marks for the legs – both head and foot – and the hole for the hinge bolt for the head of the lounger. Using the template, draw the curve on the bed sides.

Take the clamps off and pencil in clearly on both sides of the timber where everything goes. The great advantage of marking out in pairs is that you know that all the different bits will line up when you come to fit them together.

3 Decide on the diameter of the coach bolts for hinging the top section (⅜in/10mm) is ideal. Bore holes in both side pieces to take these bolts.

4 Next jigsaw around the curved shaping on the bed sides. Before you start, clamp the side firmly down, make sure that the underside of where you are going to cut is clear (i.e. you are not also going to cut into your workbench), and put a fine blade in the jigsaw.

The fine blade will give a good clean cut, and means that you will have less work removing the saw marks later. Once the

shaping is done, work over the surface with sandpaper.

5 Now mark out the four legs and cut them to length. Clamp them together and pencil in where the stretcher rails go.

On two of the legs only, pencil in the axle hole.

Cut to length the two blocks for the wheel axle. These provide extra strength and stability for the axle, which goes right through them as well as the legs.

Screw the blocks in place and bore the axle holes. It is best to buy the set of wheels and axle that you are going to use before boring the axle hole.

6 Now screw the bed foot rail in place. It is not possible to fit a rail at the head of the lounger as the folding head-rest fits on to the frame here so an extra stretcher rail is glued and screwed on to the underneath of the frame to secure this end section.

This job is easier if you have an assistant and you can assemble the project on a flat surface. It is important that you check the bed frame is square. The most accurate method is to use a thin batten and position it across the diagonals of the frame. If the frame is skewed you can lean on one corner, with your assistant holding the frame at the other, to get it square. Do this before the glue cures and double-check for squareness with the batten.

7 Once the main frame is made, the legs can be screwed in place. Glue and screw them to the side of the frame.

8 Add the side stretcher rails to the legs, and then the cross rails, this braces the legs in all directions.

HEAD-REST

The adjustable head-rest is now made up. I have used wider planks for this than those on the main bed as they are more comfortable for your head. This section has twelve pieces: five planks, two head support rails, which the planks are screwed to, two prop rails and one dowel rod, and the two slotted rails, which enable the height of the head-rest to be adjusted.

1 Clamp together the two rails that will form the plank supports and drill holes in the ends to take the coach bolt that holds the head-rest unit to the main bed. These holes need to be of the same diameter as those bored earlier (Bed, step 3).

2 Referring to the diagram, bore a further hole mid-way along each rail to take the coach bolt that attaches the prop rails, and at the top end make a slotted hole in each to take the dowel assembly.

The slotted hole needs some care. Careful marking out is the key to success. First pencil in the area you have to cut out, next use a large flat bit in an electric drill to bore the hole and finally, with the timber firmly clamped down, use a jigsaw to cut out the slot. Repeat the operation for the second rail. Studying the diagram will help.

3 On a flat surface, position the five planks on to the head-rest support rails that are to hold them and mark their positions in pencil. The rails will eventually be fitted inside the bed frame, so make sure there is enough space; you must also allow the thickness of a washer on either side to enable the head-rest to be raised and lowered without fouling the bed sides.

Bore and countersink holes in the rails to take the planks. The fifth plank fits on the end of the head-rest.

4 Bore the prop rails at one end to take the dowel rod. At the other end bore holes so that they can be bolted to the head-rest support rails. You will need to drill (counterbore) a hole sufficiently large to take the bolt head so that when the head-rest is folded down, the bolt heads do not foul the sides. It is also important to round over the ends: square ends would foul the planks above.

Glue the dowel rod into the prop rails.

5 In order to make the head-rest adjustable cut the two battens with slots to form a rack. Glue and screw these to the inside bottom edges of the main frame. The notches are cut out using the same techniques as for the other dowel rod slots (step 2).

ASSEMBLY

1 Assembling the folding head-rest requires some care. You need to slip washers between the sides of the moving unit and the bed frame – this is quite fiddly, as the washer has to be threaded on to the bolt as it passes between the gap.

2 Now prepare the slats for the bed. Use a plane to chamfer off the edges and make the bed more comfortable. As there are so many slats to be fixed, make up a 'spacer batten' (see Box step 4 p92) to the thickness of the gap. This way, all you have to do is fix a batten, place the spacer batten beside it, and simply screw the next batten in position on the other side – no measuring required.

FINISHING

It is best to keep all the finished parts separate until you have applied the wood-care product (see p18) as it is both difficult and frustrating attempting to get the brush between the many folding parts.

PLANT STAND

Potted plants of all shapes, sizes and varieties always benefit from being displayed well. This plant stand is designed to allow for large potted plants as well as smaller ones. The bottom and second tiers are strong enough for heavy plants. The second tier is supported by legs on the under shelf to give extra strength and has a curved rail to provide more space for the taller plants. The two top tiers are ideal for smaller plants. All the shelves have backs to prevent any pots becoming dislodged and falling to the ground.

124

Difficulty Rating

Dimensions
Height   45in (1143mm)
Width   42in (1067mm)
Depth   15in (381mm)

Design Tip
There are quite a number of shelves to this project, so do study the plan carefully to make sure that you do not get any of them confused. The front slats of the shelves and the shelf backs are rounded off. The radius is not critical; draw around a small paint tin, then use a coping saw to cut off the square end. Smooth with a surform tool.

Tools
Pencil, expanding rule, clamp, Jetcut panel saw, coping saw or jigsaw, surform tool, drill, drill bits and countersink, screwdriver.

Sundries
Zinc-plated supascrews (1½in/38mm No. 8), glue, sandpaper, wood-care product.

Cutting List

Back legs	2	42½ x 2 x 2in (1080 x 50 x 50mm)
BOTTOM SHELF		
Front legs	2	12 x 2 x 2in (305 x 50 x 50mm)
Slats	3	42½ x 3½ x ⅞in (1080 x 89 x 22mm)
Shelf back	1	42½ x 3½ x ⅞in (1080 x 89 x 22mm)
Front shelf support	1	36 x 3½ x ⅞in (915 x 89 x 22mm)
Back shelf support	1	36 x 3½ x ⅞in (915 x 89 x 22mm)
Side shelf supports	2	13¼ x 3½ x ⅞in (337 x 89 x 22mm)
MIDDLE SHELF		
Middle legs	2	15 x 2 x 2in (381 x 50 x 50mm)
Slats	2	42½ x 3½ x ⅞in (1080 x 89 x 22mm)
Shelf back	1	42½ x 3½ x ⅞in (1080 x 89 x 22mm)
Front shelf support	1	36 x 3½ x ⅞in (915 x 89 x 22mm)
Side shelf supports	2	9 x 3½ x ⅞in (229 x 89 x 22mm)
TOP SHELVES		
Slats	2	42½ x 3½ x ⅞in (1080 x 89 x 22mm)
Shelf back	1	42½ x 3½ x ⅞in (1080 x 89 x 22mm)
Front shelf support	1	36 x 3½ x ⅞in (915 x 89 x 22mm)
Side shelf supports	2	7¼ x 3½ x ⅞in (184 x 89 x 22mm)

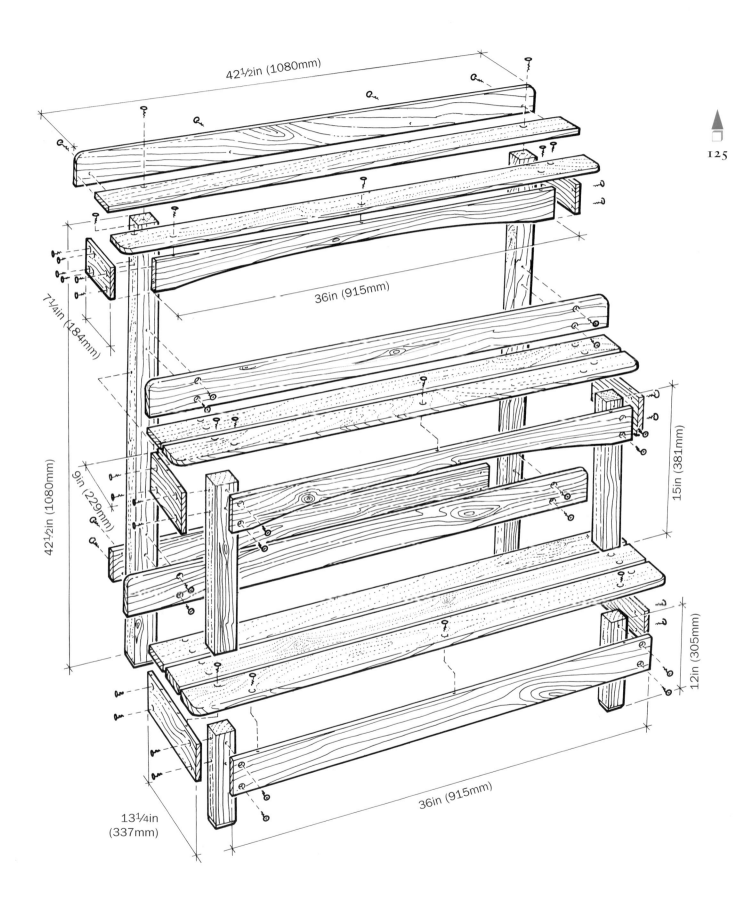

42½in (1080mm)

36in (915mm)

7¼in (184mm)

42½in (1080mm)

9in (229mm)

15in (381mm)

12in (305mm)

13¼in (337mm)

36in (915mm)

Construction

1 Start by marking out the two long back legs, pencilling in exactly where the six side shelf supports will go.

2 Make all the side shelf supports, drill and countersink the holes, noting that the top shelf support has six holes bored in it, two pairs of holes at one end and two single holes at the other. This is to give it extra strength as the top shelf does not have a front leg. Now glue and screw all the shelf supports on to the back legs. At this point you should have two back legs each resembling a three-armed signpost.

3 Next attach the front legs to the bottom shelf supports.

Make sure that you allow for the thickness of the front shelf support by setting back the leg – try it for fit before screwing in place. Once both front legs are positioned, screw on the front shelf support. Remember to use glue on all of these joints.

4 The three bottom shelf slats and bottom shelf back can now be screwed into position. You will find it helpful to make up a 'spacer batten' (see Box step 4 p92) that can be used to represent the gap between the slats, as this will obviate the need to measure each time. Before the front slat is fixed, round off its front edges (see Design Tip). The top of the shelf back is also rounded off.

5 The second shelf legs rest on the slats beneath and are glued and screwed on to the side shelf supports. Set the legs back to allow for the thickness of the front shelf support (as in step 3).

6 Before being attached, the front shelf support is shaped to allow for the height of plants on the shelf beneath. The simplest

method for marking this out is to make a template (see p16), then transfer the shape on to the timber. Cut it out with a coping saw or jigsaw and use sandpaper to smooth off the curve.

7 Screw the two shelf slats and the shelf back in place (as in step 4).

8 The front support for the top shelf is shaped in exactly the same way as the support beneath (see step 6). It is then glued and screwed between the two top side shelf supports.

9 The lower top shelf slat is now glued and screwed in place: remember to shape the corners (see Design Tip).

10 The upper top shelf slat is screwed to the top of the back legs, and then its back is, in turn, attached to it by screws. Once again smooth off the corners (see Design Tip).

FINISHING
Use a wood-care product as described on p18.

SUPPLIERS

All of the timber, tools and other equipment for the projects in this book can be obtained from good timber merchants, hardware stores and DIY stores. The addresses are given below of the companies that provided me with the materials and equipment for this book.

Nordic Timber Council, 33 Rosebury Road, London N10 2LE, tel: 0181 365 2700

T. Butt & Sons, Timber Merchants, The Wharf, Stroud, Gloucestershire GL5 3JB, tel: 01453 762194

U.P.M.-Kymmene Timber, Karby, Finland

Robert Bosch Ltd., Power Tools Division, PO Box 98, Uxbridge, Middlesex UB9 5HJ, tel: 01895 838383

Stanley Tools, Woodside, Sheffield S3 9PD, tel: 0114 2768888

Sadolin, UK Ltd., Sadolin House, Meadow Lane, St. Ives, Cambridgeshire PE17 4UY, tel: 01480 496868

Humbrol Ltd., Glues and Paints, Marfleet, Hull, East Yorkshire HU9 5NE, tel: 01482 701191

Nettlefolds, Screws and Fastenings, makers of zinc-plated supascrews, Birmingham, tel: 0121 626060

ACKNOWLEDGEMENTS

Every book and every author has behind it a group of professionals who encourage, advise and help. This is my 'team' and I want to say 'thank you' to you all:

Freya Dangerfield, Susanne Haines and Jo Weeks who patiently edited the book; Mr and Mrs G Hill, who kindly gave their permission for photographs to be taken in their garden; Keith Field the illustrator who drew all the 3-dimensional working drawings; Brenda Morrison who was responsible for 'styling' the projects and designing the book; Esa Mikkonen, United Sawmills Ltd. and Tuovi Simila who provided me with quantities of timber; Charles Trevor, Nordic Timber Council for advice on the uses of Nordic Timbers; John Roberts of Bosch Power Tools for the supply of power tools; Elizabeth Blades of Stanley Tools for supplying all the hand tools, saws, cramps, planes etc., Bebra Barker and Linda Barnes of Sadolin who supplied a wonderful range of wood care products.

INDEX

Italics refer to illustrations, **bold** refers to diagrams